SIBLING RIVALRY

IN

GOD'S FAMILY

By: Elmer Morgan

ISBN-1-56794-033-1

BIBLE & TRACT CORPORATION
P.O. Box 821220   Fort Worth, Texas 76182

DEDICATION

With deep esteem this book is dedicated to Robert G. Neil, in expression of thankfulness to God for his love for me through the years. As my father in the faith, he not only taught me the way, but encouraged me to walk therein.

For his long, gifted, faithful ministry I am grateful, and for the thousands he has touched for God along the way, not a few of whom are in full time Christian service around the world.

TABLE OF CONTENTS

Bible quotations are from the New International Version unless otherwise stated.

FOREWORD

This book is about the delicate and touchy problem of the place and importance of fellowship amid relationships in the church. It is significant because the question of proper love and respect for each other is paramount in the family of God. This book deals with the reality that comes very close to being the formidable fence over which honest, sincere brethren of differing views eye one another with doubt and suspicion.

Among the fussing and fighting of Paul's time, he lovingly advised in II Cor. 12:15 that he would very gladly spend for them everything he had and expend himself as well. Our day reveals much unhappiness and restlessness in the church. We, today, are experiencing the need for greater dedication on the part of the pulpit and the pew.

This book is for the realist who is willing to admit something is wrong. We do not pretend to give relevant and practical answers to every question.

This book is designed to motivate you to ask questions and go searching for the answer.

The world is perishing for lack of knowledge of God and the church is famishing for want of His presence. Not until we in the church are aware of the presence of the almighty, and realize we are here only to do His bidding, will our impurities be burned from our lives.

This effort to produce grist for your mill has been made in the hope that our humble grinding together will sharpen our sensitivity to the vulnerability and hurt of others. May our shepherds have a renewed concern for the sheep who are often mistakenly called wolves by some.

If we, through our interest in others, desire to keep alive the flow of communication between the devout and the disgruntled, we cannot ignore nor take a negative attitude toward their problems.

Perhaps the greatest psychological, spiritual, and medical need we have today is the need for hope. May God bless this little book to that end as we strive for a better understanding of each other.

INTRODUCTION

"Times Square, fully lit, would be a magnificent sight, if only one could not read," so said G.K. Chesterton. The same might be said of the church today in all of its busy business. To maintain this bright spectacle we have had to turn our attention to about everything but preaching the gospel and going in great numbers to the lost of the world. Mission work has been replaced with building payments and preaching is a bore. Untouched by national tragedy and untainted by deep study, we are about as exuberant about our religion as most other things.

Many of us who are professionally part of religion in America are less than impressed by the bright lights. Perhaps that is because we can read, and we are embarrassed by the messages we do proclaim. We see things being done in the name of Christ today that make us ashamed. The pews are empty and the plain message is one of health, wealth, happiness, and maybe even justice. Christianity, as we know it today, is being packaged for a market that seems infinitely various in its demands. It offers fellowship, liberation from political oppression, and psychological depression. It is better for you and costs you nothing. Your state of mind from frustration to self-image is the most important. To think of doing anything, or preaching anything, that might prick the heart of someone whom you love is unbearable.

We have been taught that the church is the family of God, the body of Christ, of which He is the head, a light set on a hill, the people of God, the salt of the earth and the light of the world. We who can read know that we are, as Paul put it in I Cor. 4:1, stewards of the mysteries of God. Stewards of God are seen as salesmen to the markets, and some of us are profoundly uneasy of all that says. We believe that the church is a community of people called to serve at the foot of the cross. We are called to give, serve, pray, even die for the cause of the gospel. To believe this with conviction today may cause one to be thought of as radical. It may cause you to find your public relations damaged and your budget unbalanced. You may even be called upon to suffer many unpleasantries, even persecution and maybe imprisonment, or even execution by your own brethren. It has been known to happen.

In the market place today, the church that once was known as the mainline is more aptly called the old-line and is fast becoming the sideline. The demand for change is so great that many church leaders are running scared. You see, in today's church the only two things that really mean anything anymore are attendance and contribution. As long as that is on the upswing things are in good shape. When that goes down, out goes the preacher. A scapegoat is all we need and he is it. The courage of a man to stand for the truth and carry the load of ministry in saving the lost is no longer important in the social church.

Some elders today no longer worry about sheep that have no shepherd. They are not running around with a Bible in their hand seeking the lost. They have a copy of the budget and the checkbook in their hand. Truth is, it is not their business, or anyone else's, how much you give to God. It is not their business to tell you what to give. It's their business to know that you know what the Lord wants you to know from His word about stewardship, and to excite you about your support of the local work at home. How would you raise the needed money to support a good work? Prod, urge, seduce, threaten, force, beg, plead, there are ways; but God's way is teaching and communicating. Make known the need as best you can and appeal with love for the assistance to get it done.

How should we live in the family as we either solve the problem or contribute to it?

In a sense, we call the people of the whole world the human family. We realize the distinction of the individual family but in this book we are studying the relationship of siblings or brothers and sisters in God's family. It is no secret that family life includes a measure of conflict, even so we learn to live with each other and accept and appreciate each other as we grow spiritually together in the church. We are astonished by the intensity and durability of conflicts that are brought into the church from experiences that happened outside the church. As we learn to forgive and accept each other, our differences, roles, and developmental stages become far less significant and diminish these conflicts as we grow together. Our adult sibling conflicts are often derived from the child still deep inside us, but as mature Christians, we must realize that jealousy and competitiveness with each other in the Kingdom is not acceptable before the Lord. We would think as we grow spiritually that these difficulties and questionable practices would diminish.

We do not hear in these degenerate days the accepted view held by many that the letters to the seven churches in Asia depict seven stages in the history of the church. We would agree that if that is so, then surely we are living today in the <u>lukewarm</u> stage, neither cold nor hot. Many pride themselves on having reached that stage in life. They are not extremists. They have reached the happy medium. They are so moderate in their view and tolerant and inoffensive regarding the views of others. The Lord declares that such folks make him sick. When we become so completely possessed with negativism and become so apathetic that we have nothing for which to stand, we are then motivated to shut our eyes for fear of seeing what is wrong and hold our tongue for fear of being offensive. We sit by the fire nursing ourselves in a half sleep believing that in this day nothing is necessary except the great sacred principal that "nothing is necessary". We believe now that love could not exist were it not for this kind, compassionate, sympathetic attitude.

Toleration of error and compromise with the world has proven fatal. The church has ceased to fight. We have allowed the enemy to triumph and are now fast dying out. Real Christianity is aggressive. It declares war on all error and sin. Other religious systems compromise with wrong, but New Testament Christianity opposes the world, the flesh, and the devil. In this opposition there is always the possibility of conflict. There are those who would disagree with out methods, and values in opposing that which is wrong. Our knowledge or lack of knowledge of the scriptures, maybe even attitudes that have gone sour may contribute to conflict. If each of us, as members of the church, could realize that we are but soldiers enlisted to fight the good fight of faith, led by him who goeth forth conquering and to conquer, what a difference that would make. Instead of being filled with criticism, opposition, jealousy, pride and vanity, we would equip ourselves with the whole armor of God to fight the good fight of faith. Instead of being filled with well-equipped soldiers eager to fight, many congregations today seem to be like hospitals for the sick and the in-firm. It is certain that if we refuse to fight, we must prepare to die. For the enemies of the Lord and his Word do not cease their efforts to destroy us. If we are real Christians, we must be aggressive. An army always on the de-fensive wins no great victory. Churches content with merely holding the fort will one day discover there is no fort to hold. When you are in the battle launching an offensive for the right, you develop critics. These are the ones with whom conflict will arise.

Sibling rivalry in God's family covers many topics. While you may not find your particular situation here, you may discover that the techniques and skills described are applicable to your own experiences. The goal of this book is to help us to better understand sibling rivalry in the church and how that conflicts, jealousies, and competitiveness arise among members. Conditions and situations often make their contribution to the negativism or opposition which one encounters.

At the time Jesus was born, Palestine was ruled by the Herods under the Romans. As soon as the Jews realized that Jesus had not come to lead a Jewish army in revolt against Rome, most of them forsook him. In about three years after Jesus began his public ministry, the leaders of the Jews incited the mob and intimidated the Roman governor to the extent that they got him crucified. Then in about forty years, A.D. 70, they rebelled against Rome. Jerusalem was captured after a few months of siege. The temple was torn down until not one stone was left upon another. This fulfilled the prophecy of our Lord. In the suppression of the rebellion, the Romans killed nearly two million of the Jews and sold the survivors in the slave markets of the world until the buyers would no longer buy. In a few years, a false Messiah, pretending to be Christ, led the Jews in another short rebellion. After furious and bloody fighting, this too was put down.

Conditions and situations make their contribution to those who do not understand or whose preconceived ideas will not allow them to accept reality. Each member has a perfect right to his own opinion and everyone can make a contribution to our success. The conclusion is that unless we are going forward, we are going backward. Unless we are growing, we are dying. He, who sows no seed, has no harvest. You send no ships out, you have no ships come in. In the face of reality there will always be the opposition syndrome with which to deal. This book is designed to help us further understand the problems we encounter in trying to run faithfully the race before us.

There will always be mountains in the path of the person or church that is trying to do God's will. If you can't, through prayer, remove them; then climb them, and with God's help go on to greater things. I have observed that the people who have made a real impact on my life were those who through failure and loss didn't stop, but kept on going. They didn't listen to the people who didn't agree with them, but kept looking for the answer they needed. Conflict will always be there, critics will be loud in negative opposition to any plan to win. The difference in the winner and the loser is that the winner fell, but had the courage to get up and try again. That's what this book is all about. We will take a real, long, hard look at why conflict arises and what real Christians should do about it. I have learned that if you are determined to carry the ball, Satan will see to it that you will be tackled.

1

RELATIONSHIPS

Interpersonal relationships with those of the same congregation to which one belongs plays a very important part in the satisfaction gained by being a member there. We hear more and more now-a-days about friendship evangelism. The emphasis seems to be on a lifestyle that meets, at least in part, the social demands also. Some 80 or 90 percent of all converts are influenced by a relative or close personal friend. Moreover, the growth in Christ we all desire comes also through a process in which Christians share their lives with one another.

In contrast to the modern emphasis on rugged individualism, the Bible places emphasis on the things we do for one another. Christian fellowship is so important and precious that the most severe discipline the church can mete out on one is to withdraw that fellowship.

Here are some scriptures that show God's emphasis on the importance of how we feel about each other.

"Greet one another" (Rom. 16:16),

"Accept one another" (Rom. 15:7),

"Offer hospitality to one another without grumbling" (I Peter 4:9),

"Love one another" (Rom. 13:8),

"Be devoted to one another in brotherly love" (Rom. 12:10),

"Honor one another among yourselves" (Rom. 12:10),

"Each member belongs to all the others" (Rom. 12:5),

"Equal concern for each other" (I Cor. 12:25),

"Serve one another" (Gal. 5:13),

"Uses whatever gift to serve others" (I Peter 4:10),

"Be kind and compassionate to one another" (Eph. 4:32),

"Forgiving each other" (Eph. 4:32),

"Bear with one another in love" (Eph. 4:2),

"Have fellowship with one another" (I John 1:7),

"Carry each other's burdens" (Gal. 6:2),

"Submit to one another (Eph. 5:21),

"Instruct one another" (Rom. 15:14),

"Speak to one another in psalms, hymns, and spiritual songs" (Eph.5:19),

"Confess your sins one to each other" (James 5:16),

"Pray for each other" (James 5:16),

"Encourage one another" (II Thes. 5:11),

"Spur one another on toward love and good works" (Heb. 10:24),

"If you keep on biting and devouring each other, watch out or you will be destroyed by each other" (Gal. 5:15).

In the light of scriptural witness, we must accept the belief that each and everyone of us is created to manifest God's glory. We do this best when we submit to God's will with intent to serve God's good pleasure. He who knows God's word is able to know God's will for his life to a greater measure than one who does not know the Bible.

Our dealings with others shape our beliefs about them. Using people for one's own personal gain is wrong. A Christian can become derailed when jealousy, envy, hate, anger etc. are allowed to possess the heart. Nothing justifies letting the heart turn on another for selfish reasons. It is certain that when a determinative attack is made on another, the scene behind the scene needs investigating. Action is caused and valid or not, there are reasons as to why war has been declared. Difficult problems often arise between Christians that seem puzzling only because all the truth has not been told.

To get this chapter in proper perspective, I wish you would stop right now and read First John. This short book will help to draw a better picture of the relationship we should have with our brethren, peers and fellow members in general.

Now! May I ask, in the light of that book, how much responsibility toward another is realistic, fair and right? Determining this degree of responsibility is a great problem because, here not only is our spirituality being affected, but salvation of one or more could be at stake. There is a need also to define a balance point of one's sense of comfort. There may well be some options, but the question is, what are they and which one is best? Any option that God will accept is better than one outside of His will, but just because such an option is not wrong, doesn't mean it is the best one to choose. We are concerned as to what is best for the long haul, not just for the moment.

The extraordinary way we are taught in the Bible to deal with the problem is surely the best way. Read Matt. 18:15-17 as a guide to help in a time of friction and disappointment.

> "If your brother sins against you, go and show him his fault, just between the two of you. If he listens to you, you have won your brother over. But if he will not listen, take one or two others along, so that every matter will be established by the testimony of two or three witnesses. If he refuses to listen to them, tell it to the church; and if he refuses to listen even to the church, treat him as you would a pagan or a tax collector."

The dominant view of the Christian is that we all are made in the "image of God" and the way we feel about each other is very important.

At times our feelings surface and, in spite of all we know or believe, dominate us, at least for a while. We can feel anxious, ashamed, bored, envious, tired, guilty, proud, good or bad. What about when we are upset, hurt or feel we have been used?

Like the dash of a car, there are indicators that can serve to warn us of some external danger that sometimes we sense but can't explain. This unique emotion is easily communicated to another even without our knowing it, a look, tone of voice, etc. Body language is powerful. Sometimes a person is quite irritable without really knowing why. When we lose control, anger frequently emerges and often to our surprise. Circumstances can supply the stimuli that causes the reaction with which we now must deal. That special kind of fear called apprehension can threaten behavior patterns and cause guilt or depression. This drives us to the place that only forgiveness will suffice. This produces an unstable condition where one is vulnerable and sensitive to the situation and should take caution before making a decision.

Rivalry among siblings in God's family can be as real as in any other family. If threatened sufficiently, one can be convinced the congregation would be better off without them. This forces one near the edge of the cliff where any move, or a wrong move by anyone, could be fatal. Unquestionably, a situation like this needs a particular stroke of tender loving care on the part of all involved. In this setting, a clique or group can be formed with no intention of wrong doing which can result in real problems later down the line. In a perturbed state of mind, one is at the mercy his emotions and some people are experts at playing with the emotions.

It is here one can experience the most painful of all emotions, that of being used. The joy of helping others is one of the great satisfactions of life, but when you have been provided this pleasure and joy only to see later you were taken advantage of and used, your trust and confidence falters. When one has been deceived, lied to and used, or it becomes obvious one is more interested in what we can do for them than they are in us, the whole human race slides down a notch.

Abandoned in our own self pity we wonder if we will ever get over it. What do you do with a horrible, bad smelling wound? You dress it, care for it, though healing may be slow, and everyone doesn't heal at the same speed. Don't lose faith in God or blame the church. Survival is the point of concern now. You simply cannot allow yourself to be pushed over the cliff. Hercules cannot help you now. It is up to you. Deep inside is the faith that will see you through.

Delusions, fears, pity, sorrow are all for naught because people are people, and always will be. Jesus compounded the love of God when he chose to give His life for us. It is to Him we owe it all. "The love of God constraineth us."

When one needs our knowledge, advice, esteem, and love, it is a compliment to us; and the privilege of service in the Kingdom is the greatest of all callings. It is not the worst thing occasionally to be used, even in the worst sense. The worst thing is to never be needed, wanted or used at all. A potential exploitation can be a real answer to prayer when you are so lonely you could die.

I cannot tell you why a prayer that has been prayed for ten years is answered on the one thousandth request, when God has met the first 999 with silence, but I can tell you how wonderful it is to be loved and needed by someone, somewhere, sometime.

2

WHY DO WE
FIGHT
EACH OTHER

It was a dark night, outside and inside. Friction was so thick you could cut it with a knife. Elders that had worked on the same team for quite a while, though not together, were now coming down to the wire. In this elders' meeting, decisions would be made that would determine the future of the congregation for years to come, and affect the salvation of souls in ways these men had not as yet even thought of.

The church, of all places, should be a place of love and peace. Men should care about the future of the church and the "peace of God that passes all understanding." Souls are at stake here. Salvation is a serious matter. Jesus warns us in Matt. 18:6,

"But if anyone causes one of these little ones who believe in me to sin, it would be better for him to have a large millstone hung around his neck and to be drowned in the depths of the sea."

If we can't get along in the church as brothers in Christ doing God's work to God's glory - how will we be happy together in heaven?

Tonight, these were not the questions or thoughts that had surfaced. This meeting had turned into a battle of wills. Not a battle of right and wrong. Not a battle of what was best for the church. Not a battle of doing what God wanted to God's glory. Not a battle of conviction. Not a battle for the minds of men. It was a power struggle. It was a battle "to get my way", whatever the cost.

The meeting had become a battleground of words. Insults, sarcasm, resentfulness and bitterness showed themselves in every expression. What the past had done in the hearts of these present had become obvious as each man struggled to gain an advantage over the opposition. Grown men acting as if there were no rules to go by.

I wonder, in my weak knowledge of church history, if this attitude didn't dominate the meetings that resulted in major splits in the church in the past.

It wasn't a matter of right or wrong so much as it was, "Who are you to say we can't have it or do it," compared to those who said, "Who are you to say you can?"

James, the physical brother of Jesus, and an elder in the Jerusalem church, gives us some insight from the Holy Spirit.

> "What causes fights and quarrels among you? Don't they come from your desires that battle within you? You want something but don't get it. You kill and covet, but you cannot have what you want, you quarrel and fight. You do not have, because you do not ask God. When you ask you do not receive, because you ask for the wrong motives, that you may spend what you get on your pleasures." James 4:1-3

God's first answer as to why we fight so much is that we are driven by "desires for pleasure."

In this same chapter James continues in verses 13-17:

> "Now listen, you who say, "Today or tomorrow we will go into this or that city, spend a year there, carry on business and make money." Why,

you do not even know what
will happen tomorrow. What
is your life? You are a mist
that appears for a little
while and then vanishes. Instead you ought to say, "If
it is the Lord's will we will
live and do this and that."
As it is, you boast and brag.
All such boasting is evil.
Anyone, then, who knows the
good he ought to do and
doesn't do it, sins."

The climate in a meeting like this
is never controlled by one's reality of
the brevity of life. Seldom is there
much praying done, asking God for wisdom, although we are taught to pray for
this gift. The atmosphere in this kind
of setting is not one of, "what does
the Lord want" but how can one get his
way.

What is the pleasure which drives
this meeting to the point of ridicu-
lousness? It is the matter of winning
or losing. It is the same attitude
that causes an ex-husband to spend
$5,000 in court with a lawyer rather
than give the divorced wife $2,000; be-
cause to keep her from getting anything
is a victory, regardless of how much it
costs him.

If there are elders in this meeting who are thinking of the good of the
church, they are limited in their ability to do much; because the opposition

is no longer going by the rule book. The aggressor has recruited everyone he can find to side with him, thus giving him what he believes to be leverage in the final decision. The question, remember, is not what is right, true or fair; the question is, "How do I win? How do I get my way?"

This brings up an interesting point as to how he gained his recruits in the first place. One thing is sure, since he is not playing by the rule book, his tactics may not always be the purest in fact or motive. One thing about this kind of leader that seems to always be an asset for him is that he is a man with much charisma. People love him, believe him, and respect his ability to lead. It may take years for truth to surface and the half to be told.

The greatest need in this meeting tonight is to refocus. A peace treaty if signed by everyone wouldn't be the answer. The next move would be in the next meeting, "Go to your respected corner." We know the rest. In the meantime, communications break down. Sulking silence prevails everywhere. We would wish each leader would accept the other with love and understanding, forgiveness and concern, even sit down together and read Phil. 2:3-4.

"Do nothing out of selfish ambition or vain conceit, but in humility consider others

better than yourselves. Each
of you should look not only
to your own interests, but
also to the interests of
others."

But they are not about to do it. The
chasm widens as the night wears on.
Discussion has more than once gotten
out of hand. Emotions show, tempers
flair, reason is nowhere to be found.
Things are said that were not meant.
Methods of winning surface that have
worked in the corporate world, but
should never have been tried in the
church. Can I make the opposition mad
enough to resign and stomp out and
quit? That would be a win. What would
happen to him? I don't know and I
don't care.

Finally, one jerks out his pen
and, with trembling hand, begins to
write his resignation as an elder; because obviously, he can't get his way.
Another questions what he is doing and
responds to his answer with, "In other
words, if you can't get your way, you
will just gather up your marbles and go
home." To this, he puts up his paper
and pen and suggests this meeting ad-
journ until another time.

In all of this, noble characteristics have appeared and hearts have been
touched. Forgiveness is granted without even being requested and with sad,
heavy hearts the group leaves, even
without a dismissal prayer, knowing

deep in their soul nothing has been
solved; and on the horizon brews the
same turbulent storm as before. "God
help us!"

The concern for the church? What
is best for the congregation? How do
the people feel? All of this is not
even a part of the planning for the
next meeting. Now we are down to
strategy, methods, moves, leverage, all
a power play in the game of winning.
Sibling rivalry among spiritual
brothers in the family of God. The
needs of others, the progress, reputation of the church in the community,
the place of leadership one might hold
in the future, an acceptable race well
run in the sight of God, financial
pressure on the church - none of this
matters. We are down to the "win or
lose."

How far one or a group will go in
such a battle amazes me. I have known
groups of the church to sue other
groups in a court of law, trying to
win. Don't they know what Paul taught
in I Cor. 6? Sure they do, but they
are not playing by the book.

We know there are things over
which all of us can never agree one
hundred percent. Our training in
childhood etc. causes us to see some
things as we do. The attitude Paul had
in I Cor. 8 is one I wish the whole
church could develop. His conclusion
in verses 12 and 13 sum it up best.

"When you sin against your brothers in this way and wound their weak conscience, you sin against Christ. Therefore, if what I eat causes my brother to fall into sin, I will never eat meat again, so that I will not cause him to fall."

One might ask then, did not Paul have rights? Did he have to yield to the whims of everyone who came along? Read the whole chapter of I Cor. 8 and you will see three things clearly in his thinking.

1. What is safe for one man may not be safe for another.
2. Nothing judged from knowledge alone is enough, but must be from love also.
3. A liberty or a pleasure which hurts another is a sin.

Sibling rivalry, whether it be in leadership or just among brothers and sisters in Christ, must never be allowed to fester. Such is not only detrimental for those involved, but it is contagious. There may very well be among members, deacons, preachers, elders - competition, envy, jealousy, resentment. There is the ever-present demand that we all march to the tune of the same drummer. Some people can't fight in the traditional armor, but request only their sling and a few smooth stones.

In incidents in a relationship where all are potential victims, feelings can be triggered by some of the silliest things. The invisible cause may carry much influence in such a relationship or meeting. If you just knew what else was involved or had been told you might understand better the whys of the present.

In this book, we will explore answers to the problems of so much restlessness in the church today. Problems of friction and instability among us. Does the Bible have some answers, or should we seek psychotherapy from those who know not God?

3

BROTHERS

IN

LEADERSHIP

Part of the family may burn with quiet animosity and resentment as another is spoken of glowingly by members who see in him leadership ability that everyone doesn't have. It is like bragging on one son-in-law all the time while never saying anything bad about the other one. Like Joseph, the favored son of Jacob, who received the coat of many colors out of love his father had for him that the other boys didn't get. Joseph didn't find himself at the bottom of a pit simply because of his coat of many colors. It was a culmination of years of bad family dynamics.

Because Joseph had been born to Jacob in his old age, the Bible says Jacob loved Joseph more than any of his other sons. This might not have been wise parenting on Jacob's part, but

Joseph certainly was not responsible for the time and circumstances of his birth. The fact that little brother was not to blame for the family feelings was not even considered in all the deep feelings that were in the family.

Jealously in the church can cause the sowing of discord as quickly as anything I know. The urge to punish another for whatever reason can raise its ugly head in the spur of a moment. In fact, those who are troubled toward another will take advantage of every opportunity to even the score at least in their own mind. Consistent animosity can ruin a relationship. It can destroy the sweet fellowship that otherwise would exist in a local congregation. It does not matter how the victim acts, the critic cannot accept him. The resentment is never directed at him for what he has done, but rather for who he is.

When it appeared that God favored Joseph, too, that added insult to injury. It made it even harder for his brothers to accept him. When one is the object of sneers, sarcasm and isolation, the self-image kind of goes under the bed. One runs for cover as a protective measure against that which hurts the most, rejection for the family (the members).

We should remember that, in "CHICKEN HOUSE RELIGION", sometimes we are only reaping what we have sown.

Our chickens are coming home to roost. Jacob had stolen his brother Esau's birthright. Jacob had deceived his father, Isaac, along with the help of his mother, Rebekah. Jacob's father-in-law, Laban, had fooled Jacob and had given him Leah to marry instead of Rachel. It is obvious the family history of Joseph's brothers was troubled; or, as we would say today, dysfunctional. Few hurts in life compare to rejection by members of your own family or church. when you have been hurt deeply by those from whom you felt the right to expect otherwise, it takes a while to ever trust anyone. Why Joseph chose to remain in permanent exile in Egypt is not really known, but he never returned home. The impact of rejection by family members in your physical family or your spiritual family is fairly predictable. You know in your own heart the role of a victim is not for you.

Adulthood doesn't always solve such friction in the church. People do not always act as they should. Most of the time blame is pushed somewhere, but never accepted by the most guilty. Joseph was a big man. He had the ability to look at the granaries and not at the pit. He felt forgiveness in his heart at the very sight of his brothers and asked about daddy. He was able to weep for his brothers, a response we all need to be able to make if the need arises. The brothers were the ones left in the pit, not Joseph; and as I

work with people with jealousy, resentment and hate in their hearts, I feel
sorry for them because they don't even
know they are the ones in the pit.
Somewhere, Joseph had learned that
without forgiveness there could be no
peace; and that without peace, there
could be no forgiveness.

There is the danger, which any
group of leaders face, of allowing one
among them to become the thinker for
the whole group. A situation of this
kind does not have God's approval, because it is unscriptural. If one elder
is going to do all the thinking and
make all the decisions, then why do you
need more than just the one? The authority for a "ruling elder" is not
found in the Bible.

I have always felt that none is
closer to the work than the preacher,
and that he could most of the time shed
light on the subject, just from his
knowledge of the situation. If, however, because he is not an elder, he is
not allowed to share his experience and
feelings, then mark it off as immatu-
rity on the part of the elders.

I believe most of the leadership I
know, in the local churches with whom I
have been associated, have a few sacred
cows they strive to keep alive, if for
no other than just sentimental reasons.
We are experiencing in the church now a
demand for change or "updating" I am
told is the word. This develops fric-

tion between people or groups that robs them of their love and respect for their traditions.

Distinctive personality characteristics will be evident in any group of leaders. Their differences in understanding and judgment make them stronger as a group. The extravagant spender needs a stingy co-worker to hold him down. The vibrancy of youth needs the calm hand of wisdom in the older member. However, intense caution should be taken to avoid the tendency for doing things exactly as they were done back in the home congregation. Though that church might well have made a very wise decision in doing it that way then. That is no reason not to consider the present situation in the light of the here and now.

The art of church leadership is not only to set its priorities or objectives, but to match the plays with the players. The wise coach never sends in plays the players cannot run. Wise church leadership tries to match the objectives with the ability of the team. This might not only help the congregation to be able to define its strengths, but draw it closer together and more intimate in its relationship to God. If the cause is worthy, then God is in it with us. Is the God we serve pleased with the decision of the leadership and the challenge they have put before us? Is the objective worthy? CAN WE DO IT WITH GOD'S HELP?

I have seen through the years leadership caught up in the "should syndrome." I watched them with their "we should," "we must," "we ought to do this or that;" but I didn't hear a how, or a what, offered as to how to do it. Many want a short term quick closure, highly visible, immediate satisfaction achievement. Whether this fits the congregation is hardly considered in the hurry to find a quick fix.

How do you approach churches whose objectives are greater than their competencies? The first thoughts of those who are negative toward the whole cause is that of the leadership simply being incompetent. Their reaction, then, is to postpone failure, because they are sure "we can't do it." Their response is to get together and talk about it; this creates depression, negativism, and leads to dependency rather than to faith.

The spirit of success comes from a leadership who knows what they are doing and with considerable ingenuity, creativity, imagination, drive, energy and determination create an attitude of positive accomplishment with God's help. To go for the objective that is worthy and that has God's blessings builds the competence and the confidence of the congregation in the leadership. Have you ever known a church to by-pass the leadership and go on to do great works in spite of them? The church can only follow its leadership. Any other choice would be considered rebellion or insubordination.

"EVERYBODY wants the church to grow, nobody is willing to grow it." I was hurt when I heard a person say that not long ago. The more I was forced to think about it, the more I think I agree. Most of us want a quick fix, a miracle grow solution, a magic trick up our coat. We are ready for whatever it takes to make the church grow, except commitment on our part, promotion, bribery, whatever it takes. What about our ministry as the church of the Lord? Who will minister to the hurting, the poor and the needy, the stranger? Who will win the lost? Who will preach the truth? What is the TRUST that has been committed to our keeping? We must feel responsible for that which has been placed in our care.

According to Mac Lynn's studies, he says there are about 13,174 churches of Christ in our brotherhood. There are about 10,000 congregations in fellowship with each other. In these congregations, there are about a total of one million members. There has been no increase of growth in the last ten years, only the playing of fruit basket turn over. In fact, there has been about a 3% decrease. We are failing to keep our own children, much less gain anyone else's children. We have been so busy in the Kingdom growing the church, we haven't time to teach and win anyone to the Lord. We know so much, we can't learn; but we never share that with anyone else. The power that was in the gospel is still there, but shut up on the T.V., and we just don't have time to open it.

I am glad I lived and preached in the 1960's. In the 50's the church grew by 100%, in the 60's it grew by 60%, almost ten times as fast as in the 80's. Half of the churches of Christ in the United States have less than 45 in attendance on Sunday A.M. These have none or very few full-time preachers. Thirty-nine percent of our congregations in the U.S. have between 45 - 200. Most of these have one full time preacher. Eight percent of our churches have 200 - 400, most of these have two full time ministers. Two percent have from 400 - 600, less than one percent have more than 600 members. These churches have three or more preachers serving in capacities that fill the needs of the congregation.

I held meetings in the 50's and 60's that lasted fifteen days. Full every night. People were easy to excite about the things of God. They loved the Lord. They wanted to study and grow in their faith. I would spend hours every day at the building answering questions people had about their growth in the Lord. I was not very smart, nor was I a strong preacher, but the Bible worked then and it will work now. PREACH THE WORD was good advice then, and it is now. We need a hunger for the word. We need to thirst for the truth. We will only grow as we feed on the sincere word of God. BIBLE CLASSES are a real good place to learn and contribute to the growth of others. Pray for our teachers and helpers. The growth of the church must come through our effort to grow spiritually. Any other kind is more chaff than wheat.

We often hear people say the church is losing its young people. Exactly what do they mean by this? Seems to me that this is not usually given as a statement of fact, but rather intended to be an indictment of the church for failure of some sort.

The truth of the matter is that the church has no young people to lose. God has entrusted the young people to their parents, not to the church. "And, ye fathers, provoke not your children to wrath: but bring them up in the nurture and admonition of the Lord" (Eph. 6:4).

The church has the same responsibility to young people that it has to anyone else: preach the word. It is not the church that must decide at what hour you teen must be in. It is not for the elders to choose what T.V. programs your children may see or not see. It is not the preacher that sees to it your children get to Bible class on time with lesson prepared. It is not the preacher that sees to it that your child does not drink, smoke, use language that would shock a sailor. It is not the church that allows your daughter to sit in the lap of her boy friend in your own house. It is not up to the church to stop your child from acting up in worship with both parents looking on. The church won't see that they bring their Bible to services or back home. Teachers are not the ones that allow the child to leave the workbook at home and the Bible somewhere else. God has entrusted the child to you, Dad and Mom. If your child is lost, don't blame the church.

NOW! WHAT ARE WE DOING IN THE CHURCH FOR YOUR CHILD????? We are spending more money on youth today than history can reveal was ever done in times past. Youth ministers with degrees from college as to how to do it are everywhere. We owe our youth Christian fellowship, as we do any member. They get it almost every Sunday night. There are retreats, camps, devos, parties, fellowships, Youth nights, Six Flags, game nights, sit-ins, all night outings, ski trips. Let's face it, they never lack for anything, except guidance from home.

There is an attitude on the part of parents - here they are, you do it. God bless the parents who care and want their children to take part in the opportunities the church provides for teaching and training. The Bible teachers study and prepare lessons that are so needed, and the parent, who brings in the child to Bible class when class is half over, ought to be ashamed. No wonder we are not getting their attention; they see no reason to care, nobody else does.

In all the cats we chase, how many of them are planting deep in the heart of the young person the doctrine of the Word of God? Are they being taught to look to Jesus as a mentor and example to follow? Are they being inspired to study things spiritual and sound? Do they know the real purpose of the church, worship, and service? God help us to wake up. If no one cares, is it fair to want them to care?

Sure there is friction on Sunday morning. Roles that demand attention cannot be ignored. Either a family is committed to God, or they are lukewarm and don't care enough. Jesus wants us to "put first things first." While you are giving your child a coat of many colors as an expression of love, why not help them find a closer walk with God?

4

A

DIFFERENT

DRUMMER

When one who has been on your team for a long time, a cheer leader in fact, stops praying for you publicly, if you have any sense you must admit a critic is being born. Because of the mental harassment endured by the preacher for some time through negativism and coolness plus that certain something better felt than told, he knows this elders' - preacher's meeting is probably the one.

Given the privilege to resign for no reason and being fired for no reason both added up to about the same conclusion, termination without a cause. Oh! There were reasons, but were they right or fair? Anyway, the preacher suggested to the elders they just go ahead and announce to the congregation that they had asked him to leave as of a certain date. They did this resulting in the call of an "all church meeting" where we find ourselves now.

A spokesman made it clear that no one was calling into question the right of the elders to elder. They just wanted them to know the wishes of many in the church. It wasn't that they didn't have the right to choose the preacher; it was that they just wanted to know what the elders wanted in a man that they didn't have in the one they already had. The response came back in a sarcastic answer to that question, "The preacher has got to go." Oh, we know that, all we are asking is why? Why has the preacher got to go? One even mustered up enough courage to state that he believed the preacher was a great part of the adhesiveness that was holding the church together. "If he leaves the people will scatter," was his conclusion, which was answered with a loud, "So?".

Now that little word "So!" reveals the dominant attitude as to why this meeting was called after the fact. It says, "if the people leave so what?" Or, to put it another way, "Who cares?" Elders may make major decisions and they may make them in opposition to the wishes of the church, but the church has the last vote. They vote with their feet.

Now, with the stage set, reason has been chased out of the meeting by emotions, anger and pride. We need to ask - what happened? Why has a good, strong church, all of a sudden, come to the place of all but exploding. Things are being said; confidences, respect and spirituality are being shaken. What has happened? Sibling rivalry has blossomed into a full grown flower. Brothers in position of leadership are hurt, or should we say, disgusted at the very idea that the church would question their leadership. "It is yours to accept, not yours to question," was a remark overheard by one near the wife of one of the elders.

What are we dealing with here? To say the least, we have an eldership that is bold. They did not avoid a situation that might have resulted in criticism or embarrassment. They didn't refuse to lead, they just led in a way the people didn't want to go. They didn't stick their head in the sand and hope the problem would go away. They did not feel uncomfortable or insecure in doing what they felt they had to do. Some elders can't move out front and make such decisions because they fear rejection, and avoid negative response to any situation that might lower their rating in the eyes of the congregation.

It may be that their decision was based on information still unknown to the church. They may withhold communication because to reveal it would do more harm than good. The role of leadership in any organization has its price. We have been told for years, "If you can't stand the heat, get out of the kitchen." Some do.

I like to think that since the Holy Spirit through the pen of Paul gave us the qualifications for elders in I Timothy 3 and Titus 1. That these men, who measure up to those qualifications, and are ordained by the local congregation, are God's men in this position. Their major motivation should be: what does God want? In fact, Paul said as much to the elders of Ephesus in Acts 20:28,

> "Keep watch over yourselves and all the flock of which <u>The Holy Spirit has made you overseers</u>. Be shepherds of the church of God which he bought with his own blood."

Since it was God who put these men in this position, it only stands to reason that the Holy Spirit would instruct the church they lead to obey them. Hebrews 13:17,

> "Obey your leaders and submit to their authority. They keep watch over you as men who must give an account. Obey them so that their work will be a joy, not a burden, for that would be of no advantage to you."

Not only are the elders warned that they one day must give an account of every sheep entrusted to them, but they are also instructed in I Peter 5:3,

"Not lording it over those entrusted to you, but being examples to the flock."

Now could this "examples" demanded be a guide for men of God to follow in the role of leaders? Are they big enough to be big? Do they see themselves as servants in the kingdom? Their office, their position or their badge gives them only the authority the Holy Spirit allows them to have. They are only called to do the will of Him who called them. Consider the pitfall before the man who thinks too highly of himself. The lover of this world, or the lover of popularity, is sure to communicate the wrong message. The man plagued with envy, jealousy or self-righteousness can never project the image needed to be an example.

In the church of our Lord, there was never provided a place for the dictator. He is, therefore, entirely out of place; there is no need for him. On the other hand, in the church there is a dire need for qualified shepherds.

In the character of Diotrophes the dictator is perfectly portrayed. No one reading the third epistle of John can but come to such a conclusion. Let us scrutinize him for a moment: we rest assured that he was not an elder that ruleth well. This man "who loves to be first" (v.9) was not willing to receive the apostle and his doctrine. He was "gossiping maliciously about us" (v.10). He was not content to be alone in not receiving "the brethren," but those who would receive them, he forbade. He even went so far as to "cast them out of the church"! Quite a man was this Diotrophes. We here see the earmarks of the dictator. We are agreed, I am sure, that this kind of a man is a detriment to the cause of the man who died for him.

When Paul wrote his second letter to Timothy, he declared, "For Demas hath forsaken me, having loved this present world" (4:10). Paul meant, no doubt, that Demas was affected by worldly allurements and let them segregate him from His Maker.

There is some to-do these days regarding what is worldly and what is not. We know that worldly things are directly adverse to spiritual things: that we are not to be conformed to this world and its ways (Rom. 12:2): that we are to keep ourselves unspotted from the world (Jas. 1:27). Parenthetically, may I say that there is likely more involved here than immediately meets the eye. There is some consternation and no little disagreement as to what I may do, what I may not do; where I may go, where I may not go; what I may have in my home for entertainment and what I may not have. To these questions, I believe there is an answer. I believe there is a common ground for all Christians to approach and stand upon alike. I am an advocate of wholesome, unquestionable types of recreation. We must have some diversion from the toils that bind us. So did Jesus before us. But he did not become worldly in so doing--so we must not either.

I believe that here is our criterion, safe and logical, to use in determining the answer to our questions. We often sing "Where He leads me I will follow"; "He my great example is and pattern for me" and we often preach "In His Steps," or "Be Ye Followers of Me." If Christ would not go to a particular place or do a particular thingneither should we.

It was Saul, whom God elevated to the kingship of Israel, who gave heed to the voice of the people; he obeyed them rather than God (I Sam. 15:24). God was not well-pleased with this. It has been the voice of the people, contrary to the voice of God, that has inaugurated the various innovations that have caused so much grief to the watchmen on Zion's walls. When we, as elders, or otherwise, become lovers of popularity, we become the gladiator without his weapon, as the runner with his fetters--useless in our endeavor.

The Pharisees thanked God that they were better than other men (Lk. 18:11). We are "not to think of self more highly than we ought to think" (Rom. 12:3); we are to "consider others better than yourselves" (Phil. 2:3). We must live the best life we can, but let us strive to remember that as long as we live, we are subject to mistakes and that we are never so perfect or so securely grounded that we cannot fall.

Let us so live that when "ever the silver cord be loosed, or the golden bowl be broken, or the pitcher be broken at the fountain, or the wheel broken at the cistern, and the dust shall return to the earth as it was and the spirit shall return unto God who gave it," it can be said of us that the church is better for our having been numbered among her members.

I do not believe there is any such thing as the authority of an elder. This is where it all starts. The eldership is to function as a body and make decisions as a body. In a meeting where they pass quietly along, accepting everything for peace' sake for fear of opposing some pet idea of one who may push himself forward, to gain notoriety, is not earnest contention. Paul advises striving together for the faith of the gospel, directs Timothy to war a good warfare, fight the good fight of faith. He says of himself, that he fought a good fight, not as one that beateth the air. When the apostle fought it was no pretense of striking his opponent. He did it earnestly, and effectively. It was not for the purpose of pleasing, by beautiful maneuvering, those who were looking on. It was to affect the party he strove with. The elder today has a fight on hand. He has earnest contention before him. What must he fight? The devil, his own lusts, the unbelieving world? Yes, all of these, but he must contend with more than these. He must stand for conscience' sake. The elder like any other Christian must stand up for the right.

Paul contended with men at Antioch who came from Jerusalem, where apostles who knew the truth were, and what more powerful argument could be used than that those who so lately were with the apostles were right? Men with the same principle were at Corinth, and Paul had to contend with them; exposed them and declared they were false apostles, and like the adversary of man, were transformed as the ministers of righteousness. These men did not come as enemies but as friends, doing things, and advising things to be done, that were for the advancement of the cause the Christian loved.

Contention is not only with those who try to lead the followers of Christ after themselves for a base purpose, but also with such as are deceived themselves, for Paul tells us that evil men and seducers shall wax worse and worse deceiving and being deceived, and James exhorts to be doers of the Word and not hearers only, deceiving your own selves.

Men may therefore be deceived. The only safeguard is in receiving the engrafted word or the faith once delivered. The contention must be with all who oppose, add to or subtract from the teaching of Christ, opposing every appearance of evil. The brethren can rely upon it that all wrong arises out of things that are outside of the Word or not in the faith as Christ gave it. There is little danger of difficulty arising from what the Lord has said. It is from those good things He has not said that differences generally arise, and against which contention is needed.

The elders are to oppose error and contend for the faith. The church in a very real sense is in their hands. They are human too and will make mistakes, but God knows they need our love and prayers. They need our encouragement and loyalty. I want to help solve the problem of unfaithfulness, not be part of it.

Good elders who stand with their preacher and encourage the preaching of the word cannot know how much of a blessing they are. It is easy to find fault. None of us would say the same thing in a sermon. None of us would say the same thing alike, but we can all encourage and pray for the church to grow through a better understanding of the word of the Lord on the part of each and every one of us.

There is always the tune of the different drummer which must be considered. God help us to be pure and godly in our motives. Divine guidance will not lead in conflict with God's divine word. The answer is not in our knowing the Bible but our wanting to live it in every situation. The Bible is not an end in itself, but a means to an end. It is always easier to build big for the devil than it is to submit to God.

Does everybody, everywhere have to agree with you on everything all the time for you to be happy? Is there room for a man to march to a different drummer and still be accepted?

I have never understood for the life of me how a church would put a man on full support making available an opportunity for him to study and grow. They even help buy him books to study. They say to him - now get in there and study and prepare a great sermon for us Sunday, but don't preach a thing we haven't heard before. Strange isn't it, why wouldn't his study and new material produce some new thinking?

Isn't it true the background and training we have reflects in our teaching and understanding? Christianity is a taught religion and as we feed on

God's word, we grow and growth is change. If you are not growing you are dying. This is true of a Christian or a congregation. The other drummer might be just what you need to spark study and reevaluation.

5

EMOTIONAL BONDING AND THE AVOIDANT PERSONALITY

For the Christian, thought control is the very heart of every victory over sin, be it pride, passion, greed, or lust. I am convinced every person should have at least one friend with whom they are emotionally bonded. I am sure, however, that I have known many people who did not have one such friend. I believe men and women in whatever capacities - colleagues, mentors, teachers, lawyers, ministers, can be good friends enriching the other's life. I think such relations can impart zest, vision and desire to go on to a better way of life with assurance and faith. Once that emotional bonding develops where trust and confidence is expressed and appreciation with gratitude is evident, then you have entered the danger zone. When that friendship grows to take first place in our thoughts and affections, someone needs to blow the whistle. I might say to a child, it's puppy love you are experiencing at this time. To an adult, we know it as emotional involvement. We don't, all of the time, have control of our emotions. There can be many reasons why we are swept off to dream land. Security is a basic one, care is another, if you believe nobody else cares, needs are met in that person that are not found anywhere else. Money and things play a role, if showering the new friend has become evident.

Victimization is a dirty word and it really hurts us when we come to know and finally accept the fact that we have been had or used. It hurts just as much to love someone that doesn't love you. Relationships are sometimes the easiest thing to develop and the hardest thing to end. I know of professional people from many walks of life that got involved with someone whom they never ever intended to hurt, but the whole thing got out of control because the thought center was not controlled. To be exploited for whatever reason is a sin that causes deep wounds, and wounds leave scars and scars seldom ever go away. Valuelessness is the bottom line or consequences of being used for a reason and when that is completed you are dropped, divorced, traded or just ignored. I might add to that, if we want to broaden this concept, the word "FIRED". Many times the word fired is translated by the one getting the axe as "USED UP", no longer needed. Dropped from the list as an expense rather than an asset.

The healing power of restraint is a real blessing to those who can harness it, but too often that power comes too late. Many bask in the shadows of hate and bitterness because a friendship developed into an affair, and later went sour and wounded the used for life. We can always remember that God said, "Thou shalt not!"; but it's not that we do not know better, it's that we can't resist.

Emotional bonding is a beautiful thing. You have a friend at last which you trust with your most horrible secret. They may know you better than many who think they know you. You have a beautiful friendship that will assist you in life for all eternity. You have known a taste of heaven on earth. I am sure David and Jonathan had such a relationship. Mary and Jesus were dearest of friends. The Apostles enjoyed such an admiration for each other. Paul and his co-workers were close. Paul and the elders at Ephesus had it. I believe everyone needs somebody sometime, and if they don't have them, life grows a deep color of sadness and bitterness. I thank God for the ability most of us have for emotional bonding. To be there for a real friend is more blessed than to receive.

The other side is the personality with its guard up saying, "stay away from me!;" "leave me alone". The basic characteristic of an avoidant personality is, of course, avoidance. This is the other side. People with the avoidant personality stay fed up with people. They run from any relationship with another that might involve them to the point of risk. These people avoid human and social relationships because of their excessive fear of criticism or embarrassment. They also avoid their own negative feelings or thoughts because they feel they will not be able to tolerate them. Does this extreme avoidance of discomfort conflict with the health of the church and Christian spirituality? Can this attitude produce rivalry and conflict?

To avoid anything that is insecure or uncomfortable will produce criticism, negative emotions, fear of failure, lack of faith, withdrawal from Christian involvement and fellowship. They always see the glass half empty and never half full when fighting this problem.

Let us look at five themes related to the notion of nondefensiveness in the avoidant personality. I believe I understand the person who is withdrawn and dislikes being in the public eye. They support, but never lead. They follow with all their heart, but never get in a position to be hurt. They are the losers because there is so much

they are missing. They play it safe
because they have been hurt and disappointed so many times they have just
had it with people and the brethren in
general.

1. <u>Suffering freely chosen
   in order to accomplish a
   purpose</u>. Jesus did it
   (Jno. 10:15,18). We
   would do well to run the
   risk, pay the price,
   suffer the loss, if the
   goal for which we are
   striving is worth it.
   Some things are worth
   whatever we have to pay
   or suffer in order to
   attain them.

2. <u>The second theme is the
   value and legitimacy of
   neediness</u>. Sharing in
   the life of God is ministry that lets go of
   self. It pays whatever
   the cost because the
   goal is worth the cost.
   One of the great blessings of Christian ser-
   vice is to minister
   where you are needed.
   Help people who need
   you. The risk of rejection or of being hurt
   again is little to pay
   for the joy of being
   able to give.

3. <u>Choosing new possibili-
ties and allowing God to
work in our lives</u>. This
is a real advantage
though the risk of fail-
ure is ever present.
Who knows what God can
do? How do we know but
that we have come to the
kingdom for such a time
as this? The price we
may be called on to pay
can seem as nothing com-
pared to the joy the re-
sults will bring. This
is a difficult pill for
the one who is hurting.
They may respond by say-
ing, "you swallow it", I
don't ever intend to be
put on that spot again.

4. <u>Vulnerability is the
next theme for the
avoidant personality to
consider</u>. I know this
sounds crazy, but don't
you just hate people who
refuse to let you in?
They have their guard up
and nobody - but nobody
- will ever hurt them
again. "I hate men,
they are all alike." "I
cannot tolerate women."
"I think all white men
are mean," etc. I love
people who are accessi-
ble, people who are open

and honest. To be vulnerable is a high risk lifestyle. There are those who will use you, but the reward is great. I really believe that choosing the path taught of God results in vulnerability. It's a second mile religion.

5. "The Dark Night Of The Soul" is the last theme. I have my doubt that unless you have been there you know what I mean.

God is not the author of confusion (I Cor. 14:33). The arrangement, design, and organization of the natural world clearly show that the God who created the universe is a God of order. The unity and harmony of the scriptures show that God is a God of order. The plan and leadership of God's family, as is designed in the scriptures, plainly show God as a God of order. There seems to be in the church today a great deal of restlessness. People are confused. They are unhappy. Some are determined to hold on to their traditions and even to make their traditions law. Others are committed to change, if for no other reason, than just for change sake. There seems to be a resentfulness on the part of some in the body toward the leadership. There seems to be questionable acceptance on the part of some toward the pulpit. There is the rivalry among the siblings of youth in response to the maturity of the older membership. Adult classes now are divided not according to curriculum or need for study in a particular area, but age group distinction. The difficulty of blending together in the same lesson both milk and meat becomes a difficulty often times not easily met.

There is the level of toleration on the part of some while unacceptable on the part of others. We have what is called the traditional Church of Christ with some to the left and others to the right. We have the ultra-conservative and we have the liberal. We have those who are not interested in mission work and choose rather to use their means in other ways. We have others that are devoted completely to mission work with a negative approach toward building the local congregation. You can expect in the average congregation of the Church of Christ pretty much the entire spectrum. You will find the traditionalists and you will find those who prefer anything new over anything old. You will find those who mistake traditions for absolute truths and get bent out of shape when those traditions are tampered with. You will find legalists and you will find liberals and a lot of people in between. You will find happy people and grouchy people, friendly people and unfriendly people, loving people and cantankerous people. People who are learning and people who already know everything. You will find us to be like the little West Texas community that Joe Barnett tells about in his tract, "What you can expect when you visit the Church of Christ", and in that little Texas community, there was a billboard at the edge of town which said, "The home of 3,000 friendly people and a few old soreheads". You can see that we are a diverse group coming from a varied background and at different stages of knowledge and spiritual growth.

We have several strengths and several weaknesses in our fellowship. One of our major strengths is the desire on the part of most of our members to do the will of God. The only problem with that is our hermeneutics and our lack of understanding of what the will of God is that we might do it. We are strong in our evangelistic thrust. People as a whole want to spread the word. we want to get out of the building, off the parking lot, and out into the traffic, regardless of the cost or the danger. We are a Bible oriented people. We love the Lord. We love each other, but as sibling rivalry exists in every family, it exists in our family and oftentimes there is a possible uprising of the youth toward the leadership, or of the woman's concept of her place in worship compared to what she chooses to call the traditional place of women in worship, even rivalry in the leadership.

God made us in such a way that we do nothing without purpose. Our every action depends on a reason for it. Each word we speak corresponds to a motive. Our very thought has a reason for its existence.

> "Why do you call me Lord, Lord and do not do what I say?", Luke 6:46.

Christ questioned his disciples' motives when they acknowledged his lordship, but did not obey. The problem emerged when they were in the position of servants, but did not serve. Our problem emerges when we ask God what to do and then go our own way. God's way has two basic precepts, it is of eternal value and it exalts Christ. God does everything with eternity in view. He created man knowing that sin would be conquered by the crucifixion of Christ, resulting in a redeemed people who would be responsible to Him.

It seems to me that often we see things being done and said with no sense of ever having to give an account. I think if Jesus were in our presence in person, we might think before doing or saying it.

I have made such mistakes many times, but I am learning. One thing I decided early in my ministry as preacher was that nobody was going to own me. No eldership, no membership, no boss, no brotherhood clique, no nothing. I would be God's man on the spot, reporting for duty Sir! I count my freedom in Christ a precious thing and will give my life to have it as the Lord intended. If I find myself in a situation where I cannot act in good conscience and no longer have the freedom to preach the truth as I see it, then I will move on. I may be mistaken about what the Bible says, but I believe strongly what I think it says. I cannot allow any man to bind upon me an understanding of the scriptures further than I myself perceive them to teach. I know that before God one day I will have to answer for it all. I want my ministry to make an eternal difference in the lives I am privileged to touch.

It is easy for us to become lulled into a sense of well being. We can accept the things as they have always been and even question them. It is easy to believe that because they have always been this way, this is the way they should always be. We are often too slow to change. Jesus said that if we are to follow Him we must deny self. That is hard for us to do. Self demands attention. Self insists on having its own way. Self takes time to do the thing that pleases the flesh. Self demonstrates its old nature. Self ignores the call of God. Self loves sin. To be God's person, we have to put self out of it and ask what does God want, demand, expect of me now?

What would be the answer if the business world was called on to take charge of a body of 200 members with the first requirement to please the boss. He was never able to see all his workers on the job at the same time. A visit from a friend would prevent them from showing up, a sick headache might do it. Rain would keep many from reporting when they were expected to do so. If one dared to question the worker about some part of his expected duty, he would get hurt or mad, show his temper and threaten to quit. When friction developed in the company, he just quit and went to another company. When they had committed to several thousands of dollars worth of work during the year, and only a few remained to get out the order. Only a few stood by them to defend and help. What if their business was the very largest in the world but was financed only by freewill offerings?

All this may seem as fantasy to the business world and not in the world of reality. If you think that, ask an elder in the Lord's church anywhere you can find one, and see what he says.

"Now we ask you, brothers, to respect those who work hard among you, who are over you in the Lord and who admonish you. Hold them in the highest regard in love because of their work." (I Thes.4:12-13)

There may very well be an avoidant personality quirk in those who refuse to align themselves with any congregation. With their hands off philosophy they are safe from any obligation that might produce responsibility. Most of our strength is found in following and not in leading. We have all heard it said, "Either lead, follow or get out of the way." The person with the non-committal attitude feels better if there is no harness for them to wear.

These people move fast into the process of transformation with many admirable qualities. Their loving nature and peaceful lifestyle makes them an asset to any congregation or band of friends. Their avoidant personality has deep within the heart the belief that they are unredeemable failures. It doesn't matter whether they identify with the church or not because they have nothing to contribute anyway.

Personal criticism is especially difficult for them because it is just a case of the kettle calling the pot black, which they feel they have no right to do. Their darkest suspicions surface when one attempts to align them with a cause, work or belief. They, having been hurt so badly, wonder what is the motive? They can't see why any-one would want them in their group or on the church roll. Even in the clos-est relationships the fear of loss or abandonment causes struggles against

being hurt again. Often to procrasti-
nate in making a decision is the security they need. So they tell the
church visitor, "we'll be back"; but
they never return. The visitor doesn't
follow-up because of lack of understanding of the person. The emotions
the procrastinator is feeling lends no
support to a closer relationship with
the congregation.

We all know the importance in rec-
ognizing flaws and unrealistic desires
from people with whom we desire some
kind of bonding. It is easy for me to
teach a lesson on loving our enemies,
and I can find scripture to support the
lesson. I can also understand that
when one finds me teaching one thing
and doing another the degree of hurt
and disappointment is determined by the
esteem, respect and faith they had in
me. I have been betrayed by people who
didn't disappoint me at all, because I
knew all the time they would sell their
own mother to gain for themselves an
advantage.

To get things in proper perspective we need to pledge our loyalty to
Jesus Christ, be a member of the family
of God, work and serve with dignity and
honor. You may very well be called
upon to pay a price for your faith, but
it will be no more than others have
done. Read II Corinthians 11.

The trouble with the avoidant personality is they are continually sifting through the past for evidence of forgiveness on their part or the other person's. With this they become self-absorbed and, even though they can resolve the past, it continues to live with them as a reference point for the present. They live in the past which they identify as tragic. To gain their trust, one must show proof of many things which are concealed at first. Logic, motive, purpose, result, etc. produce many more questions than answers.

6

DOES
ANYONE
CARE?

Have you ever tried to lead
singing when the whole church seemed to
be seated on the back row? Have you
ever preached your heart out trying to
move loved ones to respond to the
Lord's invitation and not only did they
not respond at all but no one else did
either, not even with a kind word?
Have you ever been in the nursery car-
ing for someone else's children when
you felt they only were not grateful
but thought you should be in there?
Have you ever taught a Bible class for
years and felt no one cared?

Most of us have experienced giving
time, effort or money to people and
felt that it was not appreciated.
Sometimes we wonder if anyone notices
what we are doing.

If this has been happening to you I hope you will consider,

> "God is not unjust; he will not forget your work and the love you have shown him as you have helped his people and continue to help them" (Hebrews 6:10).

We need always to be reminded that God is aware of all our efforts on his behalf. The truth that God is sensitive to all we do for Christ is revealed consistently throughout the Bible.

One of the finest examples in the New Testament is Revelation 2:2-3,

> "I know your deeds, your hard work and your perseverance. I know that you cannot tolerate wicked men, that you have tested those who claim to be apostles and are not, and found them false. You have persevered and have endured hardships for my name, and have not grown weary."

The prophets of the Old Testament used this truth of divine awareness to past deeds to try to draw Israel back to God.

> "I remember the devotion of your youth, how as a bride you loved me and followed me through the desert, through a

land not sown" (Jeremiah 2:2).

"Can a woman forget the baby at her breast and have no compassion on the child she has borne? Though she may forget, I will not forget you!" (Isaiah 49:15).

The next time you wonder if anyone really cares what you are trying to do in the church; when you stand amazed at just how little some seem to share the load or burden of the work; when you watch people miss class for no good reason except they just couldn't make it; when you have worked and studied and prepared a lesson and members stand out and talk instead of coming to class; when your sermon is so important and no one seems to notice; when you give it your very best shot in children's church or the nursery and that without much notice; when you pray for a good attendance Sunday and it is off instead of up; when even those who are here seem to be out of step with all you have envisioned for this Lord's Day worship; when as a deacon or an elder, you have become the target for cutting criticism and little help, ask yourself! WHAT AM I DOING THIS FOR? WHY AM I HERE SERVING IN THIS WAY? WHO AM I DOING THIS FOR? When you find the answer to the question, you will have the reason to keep on keeping on.

Conflicts or rivalry among members are more the result of darkness than anything. Lack of gratitude or appreciation is never the conclusion of a Christ-like attitude.

God is light. God is love. One who walks in love walks in light. One who dwells in God dwells in light. One who dwells in love dwells in God. God dwells in such a person, so he is in light and the light is in him.

"God is love. Whoever lives in love lives in God, and God in him" (I John 4:16).

It is as we walk in light and move out of darkness that we love each other.

1.   To love the brethren is to abide in the light (I John 2:10). The word "abide" is not the word for a temporary dwelling. It is not used of transients who merely stay overnight. The light is the fixed residence of those who love the brethren. They do not merely pass through the light on their way from one area of darkness to another.

2.   Love of the brethren is one of the two distinctive marks of sonship with God.

"How great is the love the Father has lavished on us, that we should

71

be called the children of God" (I John 3:1).

"This is how we know who the children of God are and who the children of the devil are: anyone who does not do what is right is not a child of God, nor is anyone who does not love his brother" (I John 3:10).

3. Love for the brethren is a mark to identify the area into which we have come.

"We know that we have passed from death to life, because we love the brothers" (I John 3:14).

He no longer breathes the noxious fumes of hate, he is in a purer atmosphere. He does not wade through the murky swamps of animosity. His feet are on solid ground, that of love. He has learned to overlook the speck in the other person's eye considering the 2 x 4 in his own.

4. Love of the brethren is a criterion by which we can determine if we are of the truth. It is useless to contend that we are of the truth when we do not love our brethren. We can memorize the scriptures and quote whole chapters, but this does not demonstrate we are of the truth.

"This then is how we know that we belong to the truth, and how we set our hearts at rest in his presence" (I John 3:19).

5. Love manifested toward brethren enables God to dwell in us, that is to be in fellowship with us. As we love, the divine love is perfected in us. We must love as God loves. He loved us when we were yet sinners. He didn't base His love upon our being worthy. Maybe that is why Christ taught us to love the unlovable, even our enemies.

6. When we are partners in brotherly love, we are freed from all torment of fear. This is not true of those who are restrained and restricted by a legalistic concept of the way we must live. All who seek to live by law, or love by law, will spend their time on earth "bound in the shallows and in the miseries of life."

Who knows if he has learned all he could learn, done all he could do, or if he has climbed as high as he could, by exertion of his own power or ability? There will always be doubt and suspicion, fear and distrust, under such a system. God changed the world by turning love loose. When we do the same we lose our fear and worry of getting the proper response. No man owes me anything, so I am not fearful that I will not get paid. The secret to the carefree life is love unbounded. I have learned that where there is love there is forgiveness.

In the context, love is a positive, active, energetic and energizing force. It is creative. But hate is negative. Because of its nature, love must express itself in positive fashion; but hate need not necessarily do so. It can be just the lack of love. Man was made with the ability to love and thus to be like God, who is love. When he fails in this respect, he does not cross the frontier. One must do something to leave where he is, but he need not do anything to stay where he is. Not to love is to hate! This effort would be incomplete if we showed the nature of love only and not the nature of hate, maybe even the results of hate.

1. Hatred for the brethren (that is lack of love) leaves one in darkness. Regardless of how one may claim he is in the light, if he does not love, he lies.

    "Anyone who claims to be in the light but hates his brother is still in the darkness" (I John 2:9).

    Darkness is simply absence of light. God did not create darkness. He created light.

2. Hatred of our brethren blinds us and makes true perception impossible. No man can ever grasp the import of God's revelation until he loves his brethren. To claim that one sees the truth while hating his brothers is like a blind man claiming to view the beauties of nature.

"But whosoever hates his brother is in the darkness, and walks around in the darkness; he does not know where he is going, because the darkness has blinded him" (I John 2:11).

3. Lack of love for the brethren is proof of the fatherhood of Satan in our lives. The realm of hatred is presided over by "the prince of the power of the air." Those who operate in the area of hatred and animosity are in the devil's territory. It is useless to affirm we are sons of God if we do not love God's other sons.

"This is how we know who the children of God are and who the children of the devil are: Anyone who does not do what is right is not of God, neither is anyone who does not love his brother" (I John 3:10).

4. Those who do not love the brethren are still in the domain of death. They dwell like lepers in the

sepulchers, and like the evil spirits of old, they "abide in the tombs." It is by love that we cross from death into life. He who has not learned to love has never learned to live.

5. One who hates his brother is a murderer. Under the regime of Christ, sometimes the thought or the intent may be taken for the act. Jesus pointed out that those in olden times said, "Thou shalt not kill", but now to be angry against a brother without cause, or to slander or falsely accuse him, might result in losing one's soul. One who hates lacks only the opportunity to do violence to a brother who is the object of his wrath and spite.

6. One who does not love does not know God. He may know about God and be able to catalogue the attributes of deity. But there is a difference in the ability to identify a person and in being identified with him. It is one thing to describe another; a wholly different thing to abide in Him.

"Whoever does not love does not know God because God is love" (I John 4:8).

It is a known fact that action is caused. People say what they say and do what they do for a reason. It may not be a valid reason, but if you knew why they did it, it would help you understand their actions. If you can avoid reacting to your siblings' attacks, demands, criticisms, accusations or emotional outbursts with counterattacks, counter-demands, counter-criticisms and so forth, you will be able to stay focused on your objective.

It is not smart to get caught up in the particulars of why someone is jealous of you or feels angry at you. It would help you to understand their actions better, but to dwell on the whys and the wherefores blinds you to the opportunity of working together and solving the problem. I am reminded of the statement Abraham Lincoln made one time in regard to his worst critic. He said, "I am going to destroy him." Later, as President of the United States, Lincoln appointed that critic to a very special position in his cabinet. When Lincoln was assassinated, that critic said, while looking down into the casket, "there lies the best man I have ever known."

A young man told me not long ago that his work in college was the most important thing in his life. I asked him about the church and his spiritual life. He looked at me a bit funny and said, "Brother Morgan, I've been reared around Christianity all of my life. I've eaten with it three times a day, and slept with it at night. It has been crammed down my throat until it made me vomit intellectually. I am here to tell you, I'm through with it. The Bible is a myth, and all the Christians I know are smug hypocrites. The church, as I see it, has nothing to offer."

This talk didn't weaken my faith in the God I serve, but it did confirm what I already believed; that the lines of communication with those around us have often broken down, or have been allowed to dangle in a state of disrepair. Man has come into the new age convinced that there are no limitations to human potential. He has conquered the world and those who live in it, from the air of the cosmos to the oceans around him. He has flung satellites into space and employed them to bounce his signals to other parts of the earth in the twinkling of an eye. He has developed computers which can do in seconds what it once required hundreds of skilled men many months to achieve. Man by the application of technical know-how can produce ice in the humid tropics and warm his abode in the frigid arctic wastes. He launders his clothing, washes his dishes, cleans his rugs, and opens his cans by pressing a button or by flicking a switch.

Science has become his god who provides for him food, raiment and shelter, ease, comfort and recreation. Science becomes the object of his worship. The research laboratory becomes the shrine of his devotion, and the whine of the computer, his liturgy. This is the reason my friend saw his education in college as the most important thing, or maybe the only thing, worthwhile.

This is the environment of modern man. These are his discoveries, his pursuits, his attainments. That which belongs to other days and to other ages is fit only for the museum. Religion belongs to yesterday. It has nothing vital left to offer. This is the conclusion of our secularistic age! Science has lost God in the wonders of his world. We are in danger in Christendom of losing God in the wonders of His word. It's one thing to know the psalm, another to know the Shepherd. Jesus declared that, "a man's life consisteth not in the abundance of the things which he possesseth." Human nature is still about the same. With all its drives and motivations, it still is the way of man which does not lie within him.

I remember hearing a speaker one time discuss "Productive Fussing". He said if a husband was very smart he would take notes when his wife was giving him the riot act, because unless she was that mad she wouldn't tell him the things that were really bothering her. Sometimes it's competition, not cooperation, that is needed. People do strange things that, at least in their own minds, elevate them to the level of those with whom they feel the urge to compete.

Avoidance tactics are often used to elevate one to a position of non-conflict simply because they refuse confrontation. Rather than escalate the situation that is now unpleasant, they just run from it; hoping it will go away. The games people play in such conflict can be devastating for the loser. Patterns that become obvious in the struggle reveal this to be the way certain people have to entertain themselves when things have gone sour, and they refuse the facts. The bottom line then is that there are simply productive and unproductive conflicts, and the determining factor can very well be the way they are handled.

To prevent conflict there are some things that church leaders should avoid as best they can:

1. When there is division and conflict within the congregation, never allow yourself, as a leader, to become identified with either side.

2. Avoid party groups which would cause pressures to friendships.

3. Cliquishness can very well produce harmful results.

4. Always serve in an unbiased attitude, have a bipartisan relationship with the whole church.

5. Refuse to be used. Many times the
only reason one elder seems to be
chosen to hear the problems of the
disgruntled is because he responds
the way the unhappy want him to.

6. Many times they are involved because the offended consider them
the weakest link in the chain and
feel they can play them against
the other leaders.

7. The welfare of the church and loyalty to the other leaders should
be motivation enough to stand for
the truth and right.

8. Political romances should never be
courted although those being involved can be made to feel complimented by the attention being
given them.

9. When an elder feels complimented
by the attention of an individual
member singling him out for advice
or personal request, beware. It
may be that the whole eldership
should be involved.

10. When the preacher feels the need
to carry around the secrets of the
congregation without revealing
them to his elders, lookout...he
is in trouble.

11. Facetious flattery that is often used for getting an elder to line up with the devious member is an effective way to win because the man is proud, not humble.

12. A problem that arises through courting and politicking can be solved by simply allowing the decision to be made in the elders' meeting with the result being the decision of the eldership.

13. The majority preference is also a wonderful guide for the leadership to use in determining the decisions that effect the whole church if they are just matters of opinion or preference.

14. To choose to be an elder for one congregation, and to decide to preach for another, is a bad decision. If you had rather preach, then well and good; but you cannot be in two places at the same time.

15. To feel, as an elder, you must interpret or explain every sermon or decision for the church is a reflection on the church's intelligence.

16. One of the greatest traps set by Satan for the elder is the feeling no one cares or appreciates what he is trying to do for the church. Don't fall into it. Work for God

in His kingdom, and the other will take care of itself.

All of my ministry, I have been taught there is power in numbers. The more members in the congregation, the better. The more deacons or elders, the better. I have lived long enough, and served long enough, to know in my own mind beyond any reasonable doubt, that is a dangerous belief. Only should more elders be added when the ones now serving can't do the work. The problem of adding more elders is the "rotten apple in the barrel" reality. When things are going great and the wrong man is added to the leadership, things can take a turn for the worse in a hurry. Truth is, if you don't need additional elders, why take the risk?

The question ever present is, "Didn't you know him before he was ordained?" YES!, but men change when given a little authority. I have seen elders go through a complete personality change toward me, as the minister, once they were given what they believed to be a superior position, and that now I worked for them. I have seen them demand I preach what they believed, not what I believed. I have been given their own personal list of errands to run the next week. I have been told to send all members who came to me for advice or council to them, that they could handle it. I have seen women told not to come back to worship unless in a dress. Boys have been told to get a haircut or never wait on the table again. All these things were just a way to show his new given authority which he thought made him important; and it did in his own sight.

The worst thing about such an egotistical attitude on the part of a leader is that the church loses respect for and confidence in him. As a shepherd, he is no longer effective because the congregation pays no attention to him, and some resent him, or hate him because of his attitude. With all this, you have a hot-bed of seething conflict, just waiting for a good reason to raise its ugly head. These unhappy members are vulnerable to any opportunity to move on.

We can contribute worthy assistance by listening to our elders and not being led away by some glowing new ministry that will solve all problems. The real need is to find ourselves in commitment and service to the Lord and not to man. There will always be among us the self-appointed keepers of the flock who feel it their duty to manipulate the brethren to do their bidding. You read about these in the Bible under the title of "wolves in sheep's clothing" who by their meddling will destroy the unity of the church and stop any growth or good work being done just to get their way.

The rivalry one encounters comes from within sometimes, not from another person. Does anyone care? Yes! but only one out of ten shows it, although there were ten lepers cleansed.

7

VENGEANCE
BELONGS
TO
GOD

Last year a bus carrying a group
of civilians was attacked and fire-
bombed by Palestinian terrorists. An
Israeli woman, 27 years old, and her
three children, were killed. The
Israelis were incensed. At the fu-
neral, there were among the black hats
of the Orthodox Jews, both grief and
anger. Rabbi Eliezer Waldman, a member
of the Israeli Knesset, or parliament,
was there. With fire in his eyes, he
told a reporter, "You have to kill
those who want to attack you and want
to kill your women and children." The
Israeli military did retaliate swiftly.
After their investigation, they blew up
and bulldozed seven houses where the
suspects were believed to live that did
the bombing.

So it goes in the Middle East, and in the world in general. Hatred, violence, attack and retaliation is a way of life for far more than we would like to admit, in the church and out of it. The way we treat each other sometimes is a shame and a sin. The lies and the damage is worse than a bombing. We send people home hurting in ways they can never understand.

"If you hurt me, get ready, I'll get you; it may take a while, but it will be my delight when the time is right to lower the boom." If your child is pushed around at school, teach him to push back. Fight for your rights, if you don't take up for yourself, son, who will? In the adult world, we have learned that if you will let people walk on you, they will. If you stand up for yourself they will respect you for it. The shoes you are willing to shine may determine your promotion in the company. All this is the way of the world. Jesus came making it clear that there is a better way, a better solution, a higher road, and many changes must be made to get off this retaliation merry-go-round.

> "Do not resist an evil person. If someone strikes you on the right cheek, turn to him the other also" (Matthew 5:39)

Return good for evil. Pray for those who persecute us. We cannot act as the rest of the world. We are called to be different. NOW! When do you practice what you preach? When no one has hurt you and all is well, it is easy to have a great attitude. When you have been deeply hurt and disappointed in one who you thought was a friend, can you forgive? It is God's way of changing individuals and the world. Return good and you can sleep better at night. You will see the day (when you get old) that you will be glad in the sight of God you did it the Lord's way.

I was so disappointed in George Bush, running up and down through the land crying to become president of our great nation, telling us he wanted a kinder, gentler nation; while all the time waging one of the harshest, mean-spirited campaigns of my lifetime. The Democrats responded in the same way. I thought neither of them carried the banner very well for the country. I was sorry for the inconsistency in what they preached, and in what they lived. This is the great downfall of our age. We preach one thing and live another. It is a shame that when we are expected to come through with flying colors that we drag across the finish line ragged and torn. If our children had a better example to look up to, it might be that we would see a great change in their attitude.

Whatever happened to "it would be better for him to be thrown into the sea with a millstone tied around his neck, than for him to causes one of these little ones to sin" (Luke 17:2)? Matthew and Mark repeat this same thought, which might indicate a need to read it more than once. We might be slow to take this literally, but it must point out to us the need to be very careful to protect these precious, powerless victims who can be caused to fall by our misdoing.

Old wounds heal very slowly. There is a great need for forgiveness and a real need for acceptance through the showing of appreciation. The touch of love can never go unnoticed. We are all victims of disappointment and distrust, but we cannot let Judas control our lives. The way I live is through the power of God at work in my life. I have to make a choice. I must come to know and accept the truth of God. Christianity is a taught religion. You can play church all you want to, but until the heart is right, it really doesn't make much difference. It all begins from within us. If my friends and my critics didn't choose to see the good, and not the bad, they could never accept me. If you want to down me, you should come and tell me. You are wasting your time nitpicking the little, old things that really don't matter anyway. Come to see me, I can give you some real live stuff with which to shoot at me that will really bring me down. If it is to destroy me and all for which I've worked and for which I stand, if you hate me so much you really don't care what happens to me or to the church where I have given my all, then load your gun.

But if you do care about me and you do love the work I've tried to do and the churches with which I have worked, then look up. The bad things, the personality conflicts, the ignorance on my part to do it the way you think it should be done, the lack of wisdom, the sins and mistakes I've made all are before the Lord. He knows my heart, my love for the Lord, my place in the Kingdom and the desires to which I have given my best. He has promised to forgive me, and I know He will do it. The question is, will you? The need is for forgiveness on the part of the offended and the offender. For old wounds to heal, there is a need for appreciation of the good things and a forgetting of the bad things.

If we are taught anything in the Bible, it includes the fact that our ways are not God's ways, nor are our thoughts God's thoughts. We only know the mind of God as He has revealed it to us in His word. You can only know the mind of anyone as he or she is willing to reveal it to you. If I had all the facts I could understand some things better. If I knew what others are thinking I would be better able to understand them. To know why they think what they think I need to know what they have been told, or what they have chosen to believe.

It is man's ways to accept or ignore the wrong, sweep it under the rug, play like it never happened. It is God's way for us to repent, to help each other right the wrong we have done. This is true because there is yet another day in our future. It is called "JUDGMENT DAY."

We can get mad, hurt, disgusted and tired of a situation and run away. That is man's way. God's way is that there is no such thing as division in the kingdom without sin. Division is ungodly. You see, there is not one dispute, not one grievous contention, not one split that could not be healed if we would submit ourselves to the Lordship of Jesus Christ and love one another as He loves us. Our treatment of one another is what communicates our real heart, our doctrine, our owner. You can wear the name, hold the office, play the role, but it is to Jesus Christ that you owe it all. It is His church, His bride that you are dealing with. There is a growing tendancy to desire glory from the church rather than from God. God never intended us to seek glory for the church, but to glorify God in the church. We glorify someone else, not God, when we boast of our costly vans, buses, buildings, etc. We take pride in our massive budgets, complicated administrative machinery, desirable locations and influential people who come to fill our pews. We have a misplaced pride in our corporate assets when we feel compelled to build the most impressive building around us. It becomes easy to root for the team instead of for the owner who makes it all possible. As a result, we become more concerned with advertising the church than telling of the Christ, who is the head of the church. When we become so busy building church monuments to our egos, or becoming local church leaders with a craving to feed our egos rather than to feed the church of God, we run into real trouble. When the man with the money makes the decisions, rather than the man with the truth of the book, we are in real trouble.

In the day of the ministry of Jesus in person here on earth, provincial rulers would journey to Rome at the accession of a new emperor to crave continuance of their rights. Sometimes the subjects of the subordinate monarch would make counter plea that their ruler be deposed. Herod the Great thus sought the favor first of Mark Anthony and later of Augustus. Archelaus, Herod's son, prayed Augustus to grant him the paternal sovereignty and he was made Ethnarch of Judea despite the protest of a deputation of fifty representative Jews. The servants left in charge of affairs during the absence of their King on such an errand needed all the faithfulness they could muster. Such faithfulness found hostility in the eyes of the people. If their Lord should be deposed, loyalty to him might cost them their lives. But if they were unfaithful and their lord returned - well, rulers of that time were none too lenient with unfaithful servants. Augustus gave the kingdom back to Herod because Herod was intelligent and energetic, but he said of him that he would feel safer as Herod's pig than as his son. So, I guess that we might close this thought with a question. Could your HANDICAP be your lack of trust, or is it your lack of trustworthiness? Maybe it is your lack of dependability or your lack of loyalty? Could it be your faithfulness is of some question? Is it that you cannot be counted on when the chips are down?

I think a greater question to ask ourselves is: "To whom have we pledged our loyalty?" Paul must have been dealing with this thought when he wrote Romans 6:16,

> "Know ye not, that to whom ye yield yourselves servants to obey, his servants ye are to whom ye obey; whether of sin unto death, or of obedience unto righteousness?" (King James Version)

One of my greatest handicaps in all my life has been the one Peter said he had, recorded in Acts 3:6, "Silver and gold have I none; . . . ." I see so much I could do if I had the money to do it! I want to be used of God mightily in His service, but I am handicapped when it comes to money. Are you? I have determined as did Peter in the rest of the verses, when he said, ". . .but as much as I have I give thee . . ." That is not a handicap to me. I have never been asked by the church, or any member of it, for anything or to do anything for it, that I was not willing to do if I could. I am thankful for the opportunity to serve, aren't you?

All Christians are in the business of helping the handicapped, and I'm glad because we are all handicapped. We need each other. If there is a price to pay for my loyalty to Christ, to His church, to you my brother or sister in the Lord, then I will have to pay it. I feel the love of Christ constrains me, and I have no choice. God help us here to be faithful to our trust and to support each other with encouragement and loyalty. The greatest test is not in this life. This is a proving ground. If I have failed the test in your eyes, I am sorry, but it is before God I stand or fall.

What I am about to say could very well be taken wrong. Please try to see where I am coming from, and consider the overall side of the story. This risk I am willing to take in order to reveal to you that the thinking of some of us may not stand the judgment of others of us. We live today in the age of experts on everything. An expert is a preacher twenty-five miles from home with a briefcase; he knows everything.

These experts are telling us how the church is outdated and needs change. They suggest a new program as the answer to the problem. New promotional devices are available everywhere. The pulpit has given over from the man with a Bible sermon to the promoter with a quick fix. Elders are running scared with a fanatic desire to offset the situation. They are calling for the services to be changed to another time. Teachers who teach that which gets the appeal of the people are popular. Publishing companies, in the same mode, are teaching everything from Hollywood to Psychology, but a strong Bible School is hard to find.

We must not minimize the fact that we need carefully planned programs. I truly believe the church would get behind the Bible School if the elders would set demands of the teacher. If the teacher would set demands, that would motivate the student; and results could be seen in the lives of all involved. What does it do to teach one thing and live another? Which of these lessons do you think has the most power? There is altogether too much trust put in the genius of man, and not enough put in the Holy Spirit of God. Faithfulness has always been a big thing in my thinking, and when we fail in that teaching, we sin. How can a teacher pray, study, prepare, call the children, spend money on them, work until exhausted, and then drag in fifteen minutes late to class have any impact on the student? The fact is, many of the children are motivated to not listen because they know the whole thing is just not that important to the teacher.

Let me share my appraisal of the Rockwall Church and our experience that I see repeating itself again as it has done so many times. God opens a window of opportunity for His church. If we move through this window under His power, it is possible for us to see great results as God moves to fulfill His purpose in us. In the last few months, we have seen God adjusting the affairs of nations so that the gospel can have a free course in them. If, however, we do not choose to take advantage of this open window, then, in time it will close. Satan is still going about in the earth, and his part in closing any opportunity we may have to bring glory to God, is never to be overlooked. He can do that in so many ways: friction, jealousy, division, hate, pride, envy, etc.

Jesus warned often in his preaching, "Beware ye of the leaven of the Pharisees." What was that leaven, and is that a true warning for us today in the church? Of course it is for us also, and the leaven was hypocrisy. It comes from the Greek word "HUPOKRISIS", which means play-acting. Jesus taught to beware of that and mean what you teach and teach what you mean in the face of real persecution if necessary.

I think to live for Jesus is the greatest of all callings, and that demands faithfulness in all things to which we are called (Luke 12:1).

When Nehemiah heard of the desolate state of Jerusalem, he wept, mourned, fasted, and prayed before the God of heaven. Then, He did all he could to answer his prayers. "Faith without works is dead," and prayer without action is of little value. We can do so much to help God answer our prayers.

Nehemiah sacrificed much, his zeal inspired others to arise and build the walls of the city. "The people have a mind to work." There were some who preferred to see the walls broken down, and the city desolate; and it "grieved them exceedingly that there had come a man to see the best for the children of God."

As with the children of old, so is it now with the city of the living God, the heavenly Jerusalem, the church of the firstborn. No true Christian can view with complacency the present condition of the church. There is a worldwide decrease in membership, and an alarming decline in spirituality and zeal for the things of God. The wall of separation between the church and the world is being broken down. Teachings and practices are being introduced which have many of us calling into question, just where are we going in this age of change? Some have now revised our old cry that, "where the Bible speaks, we speak: where the Bible is silent, we are silent", to now mean "where the Bible is silent, we may speak," and that is to nullify our plea. That opens the door for the introduction of anything; and where is the stopping place?

Too often, because of our halfhearted efforts, we have allowed ourselves to believe that the world is no longer anxious for the gospel of Christ. We diverted our energies and channeled our resources to what we call "Motivation." We have become "the church building people". We are all so in debt, we can't take the gospel anywhere. As most of the elders in our brotherhood put it, "Would if we could, brother, but we are strapped with debt that will last a long time." If you don't believe what I say decide to be a missionary, and start out to raise your support and see what you get in return. Motivation is wonderful and needed, but motivation for what, is my problem.

Gratitude is the womb from which all other blessings proceed. It is first among the duties and foremost among human virtues. It is the way one pays homage of the heart. It has magical powers to turn every temporal blessing into a foretaste of heaven. If we can set aside a day for fasting, a day of prayer, or a day of worship, cannot we set aside a day of

THANKSGIVING? The heaviest debt we have to pay is the debt of gratitude. We cannot count all our blessings, naming them one by one, anymore than we can count the stars. I think if we would try to count them, it would open our eyes. A child would soon run out of paper trying to name them. The blessings we enjoy call for a response of gratitude and thanksgiving. The thankful heart knows no limits in expressing itself. There is no such thing as waste. It may be an alabaster box of very precious ointment, or a few red roses, or a note, a card, a phone call, or a visit; but it is never too much for those whom we love, and to whom we are grateful.

The joke that has often been told serves as an illustration for the ending of this chapter. In an elders' meeting, one of the senior elders asked a new elder how he liked his new relationship to the body, and his answer was, "I have only been an elder twenty-four hours, and I already hate preachers." This chapter could very well have been entitled: The Great Art of Spear Throwing. What do you do when someone throws a spear at you? The world says, you pick it up and throw it right back, but God says, you duck. Or, to put it another way, you turn the other cheek, or you go the second mile, or you give him not only your coat, but your vest also. When you courageously stand for the right, you automatically stand against wrong; and when you stand against wrong, you encounter opposition. There are always those who feel intimidated by your revealing to them their own weakness, fault or sin. It is easy to tell when someone has been hit by a spear; he turns a deep shade of bitter. He becomes judgmental and critical, especially of the one who threw the spear. This develops into a conflict, or a personality clash, which prevents that one from functioning properly in the capacity for which he has been selected.

We have all heard the expression, "get your head on straight." When a teacher or preacher tries to stretch the human mind, he often steps on toes. When you step on toes, you make critics; at least of the owner of the toes. It is not easy to lead one out of their comfort zone to accept that which they have in the past rejected.

We may seldom be able to see how any good can be accomplished by, or through, tribulations. God does not always make known His reasons, but He does want us to accept His promises. God tries our faith. God does test those who are His.

In John 16:33, Jesus says,

"In the world you will have troubles. But take heart! I have overcome the world."

Tribulation includes distress, trouble, oppression, persecution and death. The Lord leaves no doubt as to the certainty of tribulations.

In the church through the years I have been encouraged many times by the load some people carry and that with a smile. They are doing their best to be a blessing to all who know them. They are enduring some trying circumstances or are distressed because of some great disappointment for which they have no rhyme nor reason. Some are grieving over the death of a loved one, the loss of health, or the waywardness of a son or daughter. Some have problems that seem to be unsolvable. As frustrating and heartbreaking as they are some problems cannot be avoided. There are at least two ways to handle them. We can either lose heart and become bitter and complaining, or we can learn that in whatsoever state we are, to be content, knowing that Jesus will understand and that He cares. Jesus said, "Be of good cheer; I have overcome the world."

8

SIBLING EMBARRASSMENT

"How shall all men know that ye are my disciples?", Jesus questioned. "In that ye love one another." You see, if God is going to be reflected in my life, it must first be done through love because God is love; and until I can love my fellowman and be sensitive to his needs and protective of his feelings, I have a serious spiritual inadequacy in my life. We all know how to keep our mouths shut, but few of us know when. The esteem and respect that I show my fellow co-workers can mean the difference in their evaluation of me as a leader.

Embarrassment usually stems from the social stigma of having a sibling who is seriously troubled either physically, emotionally or spiritually. Even the most broadminded, compassionate people in the world feel, at least to some degree, embarrassment over their sibling's difficulties. You can feel embarrassed when out with your brother because of his appearance, or his behavior. You may feel embarrassed talking about your sister when people asked about her and how things are going. People often feel uncomfortable because they believe they will be measured in terms of their sibling's limitations. An elder that does not behave acceptably before the other elders can hurt the whole leadership. Deacons who jealously seek power or authority which is not theirs to have thus create a problem, and can hurt all the deacons. Deprivation comes from not having a healthy enjoyable sibling relationship. Deprivation comes from knowing that you won't share the positive aspects of another, that you have them in your home; but they never have you in theirs. That you go the second mile for them, but they never go the first mile for you. That you get excited about the things which have caught their attention, but they never seem to care about the things which have captured your attention. These all bring about questionable responses that create difficulties within the membership of the local church.

Almost every church has a few members who quit, from time to time, for the most inconsequential reasons. If the preacher, or one of the members, should inadvertently say or do the wrong thing, they forthwith retire for a year or two and lick their imaginary wounds.

What we forget about church members is that there are always a few who want to quit. They find church an excruciating burden. They get tired of carrying the yoke. They would occasionally like to "chuck it all" and do exactly what they want to do. But a sense of duty forbids. They have to have a "reason." So it is not at all surprising when someone quits for some hidden reason. His "official complaint" actually had little or nothing at all to do with his withdrawal. The person who looks for an "objective correlative" for his resignation will always manage to find one. The real objective correlative is that he quits because he sees religion as a burden instead of a blessing. He quits because he wants to quit, but he will not admit to himself and others that he would harbor so base a desire. It is expedient to find a scapegoat.

When someone chooses to renounce his discipleship over an insignificant or imaginary offense, there is little that the church can do about it. People, who are looking for the mistakes of others in order to justify their own desires, will always find in human beings a fertile source, for human beings are worse than frail. What we can do is to love them and try to understand them. Perhaps we can help them to understand themselves.

One person said to me, "I look at it this way":

1.   If I believe there is a God and there isn't, then I have only lost the pleasure of sin for a season.

2.   If I believe there is a God and there is, then I win.

3.   If I believe there is no God and there is, then I'm in a mess.

I call this "cheap believerism" - a faith that is dead.

> "Let him who walks in the dark, who has no light, trust in the name of the Lord and rely on his God" (Isaiah 50:10b).

Self reliance! Independence! Our life and times are polluted by these worthless idols. In childhood we are told to stand on our own two feet. Boys are urged to be men and not to ask for help, or show any need or feeling. How some long to live in their own apartment and own their own car. So many go through life to feel they need no one or anything to complete their lives. Yet, this bill of goods the world is selling is as false as can be. Little wonder so many turn to mind altering drugs. Life is so painful, escape seems the only alternative. Despite a deep desire to live, some cannot endure their present pain so they take their own lives.

How often such people see life as a "struggle," a "jungle", a "rat-race." Life, which is meant to be so meaningful, becomes only an inadequate attempt to survive. Isaiah described such a meaningless life.

> "The bed is too short to stretch out on, the blanket too narrow to wrap around you" (Isaiah 28:20).

The solution is simple, but not simplistic. There is one who can control and direct life. So many refuse to acknowledge or trust Him. Isaiah shows the folly of those who will not follow God's directions.

> "But now, all you who light fires and provide yourselves with flaming torches, go, walk in the light of your fires and of the torches you have set ablaze. This is what you shall receive from my hand: You will lie down in torment" (Isaiah 50:11).

Recent studies have shown that man's belief in the existence of God is probably as great as it has ever been. If this is so, why do we see so many with problems and difficulties? One reason is there is a vast difference in believing God exists and in believing that He. . . "rewards those who earnestly seek him" (Hebrews 11:6).

I see a lot of change in our country from the way it used to be. The dam is breaking in America. Unless there is a spiritual revival, we might as well try to hold back Niagara Falls with toothpicks. The restraints of law and order are giving away. Our family life is crumbling. Ours is a day of secularism and humanism which has been defined as "the practice of the absence of God." With our technology, know-how and expertise, we are producing gadgets that are mind boggling. The real problem, however, is sin; and science has no help, nor answer for sin. This is where we the church fit into the plan. It may not be headline news that we as a people pay our debts, tell the truth or try to live a life becoming to the Lord. We may very well go through a whole lifetime without ever getting our picture in the paper, but in the sight of God, we are acceptable. Isn't that really all that matters? Where I stand before the judgment bar of God is really the bottom line.

I think David kind of got to the place I am today when he expressed thought about walking through that lonesome valley. He restored my faith when he wrote something about never wanting; and fearing no evil. He didn't deny that he had some enemies, but even before them the Lord blessed his life.

Why did the Lord have to die? In one sense, He did not have to die. We die because we have to. The wages of sin is death, but Jesus never sinned so had no debt to pay for Himself. He could lay down His life and take it up again. We can lay down our lives, we can kill ourselves; but we cannot take up our lives again. Jesus said to some of His followers on the way to the cross, "Weep not for me." He was not the helpless victim of a mob. He was dying on purpose. He told Peter He could call down twelve legions of angels and reminded Pilate that He had no power except it was given Him from above. He died as He lived, a man with purpose. We, too, can live and die with purpose.

Did you ever get the feeling that the person talking didn't know what he was talking about or that the person working didn't know what he was doing? Did you ever notice though that if the person you were watching was really trying to do the best he or she could and that they had a great attitude; that the way they were performing didn't make all that much difference? We love people who are giving it their best shot. The teacher in Bible school who doesn't know all there is to know, but who is trying and growing, is a blessing. The one who thought he knew much more but was not committed could do lasting harm.

In 1915, Leon Trotsky attended Sunday School with a friend in Chicago. The teacher did not arrive to teach the class that morning and, unfortunately, had not notified anyone of his intention to be absent. Leon Trotsky walked away from Sunday School class, as far as it is known, never attended another one. A few months later, he returned to his native Russia and in 1917 led the Bolshevik Revolution in Russia which brought the Communist regime to power.

Bible School teachers do make a difference by their concern, or by their unconcern, for outreach, by what they will do or will not do. I am more concerned about the value the teacher places on the job than I am the fear they do not know enough. The fear of teaching error should always be present, and we all need to be very careful to teach only that which is from the book. I am very slow to take the ideas of others as law and truth, except as can be shown from the Bible. I think to put your trust in a version of the Bible that one man produced is a danger, because he will interpret it as he believes it is. If there are many working on the translation the view may be broader. I think we all are somewhat dependant on the teaching of others, but in the last analysis we must accept only that which we believe the teaching has come to mean. Can we ask God for help if we are not making our best effort? Can we ask God for strength if we have strength we are not using? Can we ask for prosperity if we have proven that we cannot be trusted with it? Can we ask God for faith if we refuse to act on the faith we already have? Can we ask for forgiveness if in our hearts we will not forgive? Can we ask for guidance if we refuse to follow in the way we know is right? God help us all to give it our best to His glory!

The door posts of many Jewish homes tell a story. On the right side of the entrance is a little case on which the Hebrew word "shaddai" (almighty) appears. Inside the case is a mezzo which consists of a small parchment scroll containing two paragraphs from the book of Deuteronomy (the Torah). In one paragraph, chapter 6:4-9, are the familiar words,

> "Hear O Israel, the Lord our God, the Lord is one. And thou shalt love the Lord thy God with all they heart, with all they soul, and with all thy might."

When Jesus was asked by a scribe which commandment was first of all, he quoted this very passage, adding,

> "The second is this, Thou shalt love thy neighbor as thyself" (Mark 12:28-31). The passage continues, "These words which I command thee

this day shall be upon thy
heart. . .and thou shalt
write them upon the door
posts of they house and upon
thy gates."

The second paragraph in the mezzo,
Deuteronomy 11:13-21, outlines rewards
for obedience, punishment for disobedi-
ence, and the necessity of teaching
children the word of God.

There are three differing groups
among Jews. There are conservatives
who accept the Mosaic Law as binding,
but allow adjustments to changing conditions. There are the reformed who do
not accept the Moasaic Law in its en-
tirety or the interpretations of the
law found in the Talmud. Moral values
are stressed rather than ritual and
ceremony. Then there are the orthodox
who accept as binding the Mosaic Law
and the authoritative rabbinical interpretations in the Talmuds.

In the Christian world, there are
also three differing groups. There are
liberals who do not object to "going
beyond that which is written." There
are those of Universalist leaning whose
beliefs are so nebulous as to allow
them to reject God's word and Christ as
God's Son. Finally, there are those
who insist upon a "thus saith the Lord"
in all things pertaining to faith and
practice.

Embarrassment often comes when there are those of a more liberal school than ours who try to speak for all of us in the church. Since, in the church of Christ, we have only local autonomy, there is no governing body to tell each church what they must believe. In each local congregation there may very well be different thoughts that bring embarrassment to other siblings because of their feelings about the opinion being expressed.

I have been asked about preachers who fell off their perch publicly, and how I felt about them. The truth is, they hurt us all. Not that we all haven't sinned, but that people who are embarrassed over their action have a tendency to classify all of us in the same group, and thus condemn the ministry in general. I am sure the reflection of damage done to each other was never thought of when the sin was being committed that brought on the publicity.

Ours today is a public world religion, made known by the media whether it is worth telling or not. I wonder, though, if they are not looking for just the thing that will sell us down the river in the minds of those who might otherwise be won for the Lord. There will always be enough Walter Raileys, Jimmie Swaggerts, Robert Tiltons and Jim Bakers to keep the tube hot with criticism and disrespect. We all fall. It is the man who is willing to take the discipline, get up in penitence and try again that wins the victory.   That is the way a man by the name of David became the man after God's own heart.

That revealed between liberal religion and conservative religion is often only known to the person doing the considering.   The same sermon may be taken in two different ways, drawing two very real conclusions, both of which are biblical and accurate.   A sermon on the prodigal son, as an example, might be thought by one to be saying there always must be forgiveness, willingness to accept one back into the family and embarrassed when a brother will not do that.   The other person is thinking of how one must come to himself and change his ways to return to the father; and unless he can do that, his return will never happen.

The application of any given sermon is never the same by all the members.   There will be those impressed and others bored out of their mind. One will thank you, another will shun you in response to the same lesson. The cutting edge of the word of God is there for a purpose, and should always be realized as a means by which God may be calling us.   Worship today in the local church is at such a low ebb (having been replaced by "the program") that we wonder the reason some attend anyway.   We have the greatest speakers, the greatest buildings, the greatest fellowship, the greatest need while starving to death seated at the King's table. The straw, shucks, hulls, and husk served for the diet makes for no spiritual growth. The few seekers of God leave, empty and disillusioned, in an effort to find him yet. God help us. We need strength that comes from a real relationship with God...the knowing of the Lord in a personal, intimate way that brings excitement to the heart. Our fire on Mount Carmel has gone out as a result of our lazy, complacent, apathetic concern to grow in the Lord. We no longer are excited about heaven or afraid of hell. We are content to have our membership at the club and if more is demanded just let us know and we will send in a check. God help us!

A Christian that doesn't have at least one person for whom they are praying daily is missing out on a real blessing. Embarrassment over a sibling is easy to overcome by the response of one who is grateful for your care. There are those in our world who need us and will be thankful for our help. God help us find them, and stop worrying ourselves sick over those who don't care about us or themselves in their relationship to God.

9

THE

TYRANNY

OF

SWEETNESS

The tyrant of whom I speak now is one of the greatest manipulators in the business. He or she may not be doing their work intentionally to hurt anyone, but they are of the personality to keep the flame burning. They are artists at pitting one member against another. They love to play the ends against the middle. They pit an elder against the preacher, or one elder against another. They are never at peace without war. There just must be a feud going on somewhere to which they can contribute. Happiness is in being miserable.

What does the Bible say about this personality problem? In Philippians 2:5-8, we read:

"Your attitude should be the same as that of Christ Jesus: Who, being in the very nature

God, did not consider equality with God something to be grasped, but made himself nothing, taking the very nature of a servant, being made in human likeness. And being found in appearance as a man, he humbled himself and became obedient to death-even death on a cross!"

"Slaves, submit yourselves to your masters with all respect, not only to those who are good and considerate, but also to those who are harsh. For it is commendable if a man bears up under the pain of unjust suffering because he is conscious of God. But how is it to your credit if you receive a beating for doing wrong and endure it? But if you suffer for doing good and you endure it, this is commendable before God. To this you were called, because Christ suffered for you, leaving you an example, that you should follow in his steps. "He committed no sin, and no deceit was found in his mouth." When they hurled their insults at him, he did not retaliate; when he suffered, he made no threats. Instead, he entrusted himself to him who judges justly" (I Pet. 2:18-23).

"Not so with you. Instead, whoever wants to become great among you must be your servant, and whoever wants to e first must be your slave--just as the Son of Man did not come to be served, but to serve, and to give his life a ransom for many" (Matt. 20:26-28).

"You have heard that it was said, `An eye for an eye, and a tooth for a tooth.' But I tell you, Do not resist an evil person. If someone strikes you on the right cheek, turn to him the other also. And if someone wants to sue you and take your tunic, let him have your cloak as well. If someone forces you to go one mile, go with him two miles" (Matt. 5:38-41).

Fidelity to Christ in our treatment of others can only be exemplified in the second mile. Our attitude toward others must be regulated by our attitude and love for the Lord and His way.

From this we learn that man's greatest right is to forego his rights; to use his freedom and blessings in the service of others. There is no religion or human philosophy in which the true secret of happy, successful living is set forth with such clarity as in the religion of Jesus Christ.

> "Therefore, since we are surrounded by such a great cloud of witnesses, let us throw off everything that hinders and the sin that so easily entangles, and let us run with perseverance the race marked out for us. Let us fix our eyes on Jesus, the Pioneer and Perfecter of our faith, who for the joy set before him endured the cross, scorning its shame, and sat down at the right hand of the throne of God" (Heb. 12:1-2).

Hear Paul on this subject,

> "If I speak in the tongues of men and of angels, but have not love, I am only a resounding gong or a clanging cymbal. If I have the gift of prophecy, and can fathom all mysteries and all knowledge, and if I have a faith, that can move mountains, but have not love, I am nothing. If I give all I possess to the poor and surrender my body to the flames, but have not love, I gain nothing" (I cor. 13:1-3).

Love, therefore, enables us to deal justly, kindly, equitably and sacrificially with all men, both friend and foe.

> "A new commandment I give you: Love one another. As I have loved you, so you must love one another. By this all men will know that you are my disciples, if you love one another" (John 13:34-35).

Lord, what is the true badge of discipleship? "If you love one another."

True response to being hurt by another is not revenge, but forgiveness. Love the sinner and hate the sin. The world does not look upon one who can do that with favor, but with resentment and hate.

> "If you belonged to the world, it would love you as its own. As it is, you do not belong to the world, but I have chosen you out of the world. That is why the world hates you" (Jno. 15:19).

He is not saying that we are not in the world, he is saying that we are not of the world.

This gives us some direction as to how to deal with the personality who is dealing with us...the trouble maker who can't help it. This person can set an

office of women into a tizzy in one
day. This man can have a fellow worker
mad, the reason being unknown to the
angered. The dropping of a half truth
here, and an unfinished sentence there,
can cause more friction in thirty minutes than can be resolved in thirty
hours. In the church, those with this
personality have two things in common.
They have TIME and TELEPHONES. The effort they make to sow discord, if har-
nessed for God for good, would grow a
church anywhere in the world to the
Glory of God.

In my study of such personalities
I have concluded these facts. They
tend to make quick judgments about
others' motives. They often feel
guilty for judging and finding fault.
The inner voice of criticism which is
so harsh and demanding prevents them
from evaluating relationships well.
Their inclination toward pessimism is
often revealed in their biting and
satirical humor.

Their "inner critic" undermines
the expressed admiration of others and
prevents them from internalizing compliments. However, outwardly they can
graciously accept a compliment from
someone while inwardly commenting that
the person is not an expert, has lower
standards than their own, or is just
being nice; in any case, the compliment
is rendered meaningless.

Their concept of loyalty is better felt than told. They have no vengeance in their heart, and want to be a friend; but they can't find one good enough to accept without competing with them. When they feel the need to compete, they then criticize with sarcasm that which they come to believe. The would-be friendship goes sour and they go looking for another.

These people are secretive and do not easily disclose their personal feelings or opinions. Fear that irrational emotions could overwhelm them causes them to keep a tight rein on their responses. This extreme self-control can extend from emotion into the realm of intuition, thus impairing their judgment regarding other people; this repression can, in turn, lead to a financial loss, or to a loss in relationship. They especially repress their anger, allowing it to be expressed only through passive-aggressive behavior, which can be particularly evident when they do not assert their true feelings.

If caught in the act of criticism or misrepresentation of others they will at once respond with a "well, that's the way I see it, you may not agree with me." "I said that for your own good, not mine ." etc. The truth is they wouldn't have you know for the world that they are competing with you. They will smile and radiate social

charm to the point you will almost believe the stuff they are spreading.

In their value system, loyalty,
integrity, fairness, directness, hon-
esty and love are esteemed with little
importance. They work toward a goal.
They don't even have the courage to
stand up for the lies they tell. Often
when confronted they will deny ever
saying it. When proof is revealed,
they rebound with a "I forgot I said
that." They lack the ability to see
reality clearly. If possible they use
the innocence of another to cover up
their guilt. "I didn't tell them that"
or "they came to me with that information," never that lie.

These brethren know which elder to
go to because it is the right answer
they are looking for. The man who is
negative or sympathetic with their
cause is the one they will court.
Feeling they are completely capable of
handling everyone's problems and difficulties they radiate a warmth that results in success of their mission.
Over involvement in the lives of others
is their best battlefield. They look
for the gossip like a rat after the
bait. They help one bundle up and head
out into the darkness of the unknown
without any fear of what it may do to
the innocent. This, we call dysfunctional motivation. It is the need to
feel wanted and needed by others. I
have seen whole Bible classes "sold on
the block" of this very thing. This,

once successfully accomplished, is a victory for the sower of discord. He feels self-sufficient because his prime psychological addiction is pride.

Strange as this may sound, these people seem to attract people who just pour out their life stories to them. They never become agitated or tired because this is the thing they like best. They never can get it all straight, and when retold by them will be confusing, but it will be retold. Personal relationships mean nothing now that the truth is made known. Nothing is now appropriate in their minds but that which they choose to do or tell. It does not matter how sensitive and responsive the other person is for his secrets to be aired, they are willing to take the calculated risk of revealing what no one else knows. They will ask any question to get the information they want.

When law, rule, custom or tradition is revealed, leaving them without a support system to back their actions, they run. May even change churches. They will have thousands of reasons why they just couldn't stay there any longer. It is a personality sickness. It is a lack of confidence on their part that anyone would understand or forgive. The truth is that they probably won't, because we believe in shooting the wounded. Kick the man that is down, and if there is anything to him, he will rise above it. Make it so hard on him that, like Judas, he will go out and hang himself.

This type of personality always represses his desires to lead in any given situation and hides behind the curtain, telling others what to do or say. He doesn't want to be an elder, he wants to run the elders from the sideline. He has many disguises and is good at all of them. He avoids personal failure or risk by never getting in that position. The grand answer for him is, "That's too time consuming, and I cannot give it the effort it deserves." In his heart he thinks no one else can either.

In reality, this person has a very low self-esteem, but doesn't know it. They look constantly for some evidence of being accepted. They are very sensitive to the response of others. They need appreciation and thanks. The gratitude they never show for the other person, they need badly for themselves. Their greatest backlash is their draining flattery and compliments they bestow on others with a display of care and concern. If, however, one refuses to take their hypocritical pretense and responds to them negatively, the gossip is immediately intensified and the war is on. Hostility often takes the form of backbiting and lies designed to go for the jugular. If they run out of ammunition, they have ways of counterfeiting the truth to fit their cause.

It just kills this personality when they discover another can see through them with their devious ways and goals. It is from this person they run, but get ready, the guard is up; and in time, war will be declared. Everything that has ever been thought of against the innocent will be reproduced in glowing attractive tones for the ear of the critic. The truth is, if you want to hate someone, there is always an excuse to do it. You do not believe Satan is dead do you?

These are the people who will come to the meeting to support their spokesman, but if the meeting doesn't go well, they will declare they didn't agree with it in the first place. Impersonal policies and general plans are as far as they want to go, until all the lights turn green, then they will head downtown.

The truth is we all have our quirks and all of us need understanding and tender loving care. If we understand people better, we can be more loving and forgiving of them. We all are at out best in support positions for that which is God's bidding. Why people do the things they do or take the positions they take, they may not even know. I know one thing though, if we can't forgive, we can't be forgiven. GOD HELP US!

10

THE

MOMENT

OF

TRUTH

If I had space, I would show you kindness as a means of usefulness; kindness as a means of domestic harmony; kindness as best employed by governments for the taming and curing of criminals; and kindness as best adapted for the settling and adjusting of international quarrels.

I speak to you, however, of kindness as a means of defense. Almost every man, in the course of his life, is set upon and assaulted. Your motives are misinterpreted or your religious or political principles are bombarded. What to do under such circumstances is the question. The first impulse of the natural heart says, "Strike back. Give as much as he sent. Dash him into the ditch which he dug for your feet. Gash him with as severe a wound as that which he inflicted on your soul. Shot for shot.

Sarcasm for sarcasm. "An eye for an eye, a tooth for a tooth." But the better spirit in the man's soul says, "You ought to reconsider that matter." You look up into the face of Jesus and say, "My Master, how ought I to act under these difficult circumstances?" And Christ instantly answers, "bless them that curse you, and pray for them that despitefully use you." Then the old nature rises up again and says, "You had better not forgive him until first you have chastised him. You will never get him in so tight a corner again. You will never have such an opportunity of inflicting the right kind of punishment upon him again. First chastise him and then let him go." "No," says the better nature, "through patience a ruler can be persuaded and a gentle tongue can break a bone." (Proverbs 25:15)

You have a dispute with your brother. You say to him, "I despise you." He replies, "I can't bear the sight of you." You say, "Never enter my house again." He says, "If you come on my door sill, I'll kick you off." You say, "I'll put you down." And so the contest rages; and year after year you act the unchristian part, and he acts the unchristian part. After a while the better spirit seizes you, and one day you go over to the neighbor, and say, "Give me your hand. We have fought long enough. Time is so short, and eternity is so near, that we cannot afford any longer to quarrel. I feel you have wronged me very much; but let us settle all now in one great hand-shaking and be good friends." You have risen to a higher platform than that on which before you stood. You win his admiration, and you get his apology. But if you have not conquered him in that way, at any rate, you have won the applause of your own conscience, the high estimation of good men, and the honor of your Lord, who died for his armed enemies.

"But," you say, "What are we to do when slanders assaults us, and there come untrue sayings all around about us, and we are abused and spit upon?" My reply is: Do not go and attempt to chase down the slanders. Lies are prolific, and while you are killing one, fifty are born. All your demonstrations of indignation only exhaust yourself. You might as well, on some summer nights, when the swarms of insects are coming up from the lake disturbing you, bring out your shotgun and go to blasting. You will soon learn the game is too small for the gun. Well! What are you to do with the abuses that come upon you in life? You are to live them down. I saw a farmer go out to get a swarm of bees. As he moved amid them they buzzed his head, covered his hands, buzzed his feet. If he had declared war on them they would have stung him to death. He didn't, he moved among them in perfect peace.

God's way is repentance. Man's way is to sweep it under the rug and play like it never happened. God's way is to make amends for sorrow through repentance. Man's way is never admit that for which he should be sorry. Man's way is to live in the pig pen and eat with the pigs. God's way is to get up and go home and ask to be made as one of the servants, feeling unworthy to be called a son.

Sorrow is not repentance, yet one cannot repent who does not sorrow for sin. Repentance is a change of will, and with it is a deep conviction of sorrow which brings about a reformation of life, or turning from sin.

You find a thief, when caught, very sorry; but when freed, steals again. He was not sorry that he had stolen, but was very sorry that he was caught. A drunkard claims, at times, that he is sorry he got drunk, but he gets drunk time and time again. The liar admits he did not tell the truth and, thereby, split the family up. He claims he's sorry for that, and tells another lie just as bad as the first one.

Jesus taught,

"But unless you repent, you too will all perish" (Luke 13:3).

> "In the past God overlooked such ignorance, but now he commands all people everywhere to repent" (Acts 17:30).

There are many verses that teach the need for real repentance if we are to have forgiveness for our wrongs. The most productive verse is:

> "Produce fruit in keeping with repentance" (Matt. 3:8).

To me that means show evidence of your repentance, which is change. If you have lied on me, call the person you lied to and take it back. If you have stolen from me, and you repent, won't you bring back that which you have stolen and give it back to me?

Now we come to the real question. What do those have to do before I will forgive them who have hurt me very much? Crawl on their belly before me? Beg and cry to me? Pay me great sums? NO! My prayer is, forgive them, Lord, they know not what they do. Dear God, do not lay this sin to their charge. If you cannot forgive them, then blot me, too, out of thy book of remembrance. I need all the love I can get, but I'm not a fool. I know some places I'm not wanted. I know some people that don't want me around. I don't have to be there either. I can forgive them anyway. But, Bro. Morgan, they didn't ask you for forgiveness. They

don't have to. They were already forgiven by me, but I'm not God, and just
because I forgave doesn't mean God
will. There may be some fruits of repentance He is still waiting for. We
all might should get out our sackcloth
and ashes once in a while. There are
things we all could improve on if we
were not so high and mighty. I have
asked for forgiveness, or suggested
that the problem could be solved, when
I was made to know the person didn't
want the problem solved with me still
around. Forgiveness wasn't available
for me. I then turned that over to the
Lord.

What about the hereafter? What
about the judgment? What about the influence we have on others? These are
issues that cannot be ignored. We need
to live in the very shadow of heaven.
If you can't stand me here in Rockwall,
what about heaven? Jesus did say that
the way the community would know we
were His disciples was in the way we
would love one another. You might have
to work that out for yourself. Getting
the other to give in isn't the answer.
Having some big shot stamp his approval
on something you have done is not the
answer. It is, WHAT DOES GOD THINK
ABOUT WHAT YOU HAVE DONE?

God's thoughts will be revealed at
the Lord's return which is one of the
important thoughts in the mind of God.
So much so, that it is mentioned 318
times in 260 chapters of the New

Testament. It occupies one in every twenty-five verses from Matthew to Revelation. It also has a prominent place in the Old Testament.

Paul uses this thought to comfort believers whose hearts were aching over separation from those who had fallen asleep (I Thess. 4:13-18). Time and again in the New Testament the coming again of our Lord Jesus Christ is held up as "the blessed hope," and the eager desire for every true believer (Titus 2:13; II Peter 3:11; Rev. 22:20). Peter's prediction has come true:

> "First of all, you must understand that in the last days scoffers will come, scoffing and following their own evil desires. They will say, "Where is this `coming' he promised? Ever since our fathers died, everything goes on as it has since the beginning of creation" (II Peter 3:3-4).

A worldly church, as a bride flirting with other men, does not long for the return of her absent husband, Jesus Christ. The Christian whose heart is fixed on Jesus, whose affections are stayed on the Lord, wait with anxious anticipation of His coming.

> "So you also must be ready, because the Son of Man will come at an hour when you do

132

not   expect   Him"   (Matt.
24:44).

Matthew 24:45-46; Luke 21:34-36 and I
John 2:28 add to the impact of Hebrews
9:28, "To those who are waiting for
Him."

How do I know the Lord is coming
again? Because God tells us so in His
word.   When the disciples were over-
whelmed with the thought that He was
about to leave them, Jesus said, "I
come again. . ." (John 14:3). The coming again of Jesus Christ so frequently
mentioned in the New Testament as the
great hope of the church is an event
that still lies in the future. Because
of this fact, we should have the
following attitude.

1.   Be ready whensoever He may come.

2.   We should be watching and looking
      for the coming of the Lord.

3.   We should earnestly desire the
      coming of our Lord.

Then we shall see Him; we shall be
caught up to meet Him; and we shall be
ever with Him. There is a crown await-
ing those who "love His appearing." It
is doubtful if there ever was a believer on this earth who knew more ex-
perimentally about the glory of the
indwelling Christ than the Apostle
Paul, yet one of the last things he
wrote was,

"Now there is in store for me the crown of righteousness, which the Lord, the righteous Judge, will award to me on that day--and not only to me, but also to all who have longed for his appearing" (II Timothy 4:8).

You are either longing for the Lord's return or else there is something wrong with your relationship to Him.

"They read from the book of the law of God, making it clear and giving the meaning so that the people could understand what was being read" (Nehemiah 8:8).

Henry Ward Beecher said at the Yale lectures on preaching, "There is no trade that requires so long an apprenticeship as preaching." He also said that the beauty of preaching was that it has the additional quality of moving men from a lower to a higher life. George Wharton Pepper at that lectureship said, "In its strictest sense, preaching is the public use of speech with the intent to reveal God to man." Phillips Brooks, in that same series of lectures, said, "Preaching is the communication of truth by man to men. It has in it two essential elements, truth and personality. Neither of these can it spare and still be preaching." The great Apostle Paul put it this way, "We are ambassadors for Christ."

I know there are some preachers you had rather hear than others. Some men are blessed with a gift others do not have, but isn't the real test the message? It is what they say, and not so much how they say it that should be the test. I read the other day that the most important thing in a Christian's life is: "THE MAIN THING IS TO KEEP THE MAIN THING THE MAIN THING." That will work for preachers, too. How do we read the Bible? How do we give the sense and get our people to understand the word of God? This is all God's business. I am not in the pulpit to win your vote, to win a contest, to even get your trust; I am in the pulpit to speak for God. If this is not the main thing, then the main thing cannot be the main thing. Jesus Christ, His glory and lordship, is the bottom line in preaching and Bible study. The sign that the Holy Spirit is at work in our lives is a needed proof. Paul put it this way,

> "Whatever you do, whether in word or deed, do it all in the name of the Lord Jesus" (Col. 3:17).

DON'T GET SIDETRACKED. JESUS IS THE MAIN THING! One of Paul's greatest concerns was that the body might lose touch with the head. Then we are victims of our own misdoings - GOD FORBID!!!

Every generation has brought before the public some great, pure, unselfish man or woman who loved the truth more than money, more than the praise of men, than position, power or title; and if put to the test, more than life itself.

These can be numbered with the one who said, "I am ready to be offered; I have fought the good fight." Many I know today, if they had lived in an age when violent death was proof of fidelity, would not count their lives dear to themselves.

The true martyr spirit has been displayed by many whose blood never was shed, they never died at the stake, their blood never stained the sands of the arena. Theirs was patient toil amid scoff and scorn, hard work amid privation and neglect in poverty while bearing to others the true riches.

These leave their mark on every mission effort I know. Men of whom the world is not worthy. Endurance is their lifestyle; sacrifice, their theme song. They have suffered, not at the hand of the pope, as did Luther, or at the hand of Nero, as did Paul. These suffered at the hand of their brethren. Those egotistical, jealous, power-hungry men who, through ostracism, misrepresented their work, purpose and motive, akin to attributing the merciful work of Christ to satanic power. Many who have gone to their graves scourged as a quarry slave still speak. By their fruits ye shall know them. The good for which they worked, gave and prayed has been dragged through the mud of ridicule and false accusations, but God looks on the heart. He does not see as man sees.

Those men and women, having drunk deeply into the spirit of the Holy Scriptures, were too big. They stood too strong, tall and straight to stoop to the petty, little things that drive men mad with jealousy, envy and hate. They were called to a greater, higher calling than the scavenger after the rot. They accepted the authority of their Bibles as their guide, and it was first to be lived, then preached. They gave their lives to the work of winning the lost, and quenching the thirst of the souls of the dying with living water.

They were driven by a passion for the saving of the lost. They believed that no matter how fine your means or methods, conversion to Christ had to take place through teaching. The heart had to be pricked, the soul had to be touched, and the spirit had to surrender. They lived what they preached. They believed what they lived.

Those are my heroes, whether living or dead. God help me to be like them. To be remembered in the same way. Whether years or months pass before I fall asleep, my tribute now is to those who have gained my respect and gratitude, for lighting the path over which I had to travel. I'm a better man because they have lived.

Jesus questioned, "What would a man give in exchange for his soul?" If we miss heaven, we have missed it all. Those, who have led us nearer to the heart of God are those to whom we owe the most. God knows that I'm debtor to those who have influenced me in the way of the Lord Jesus. To pay my debt, I pray I might effectively pass it on.

A gift is not a gift unless there is a recipient, and to pass on this incentive to live close to God, is effective only when one accepts the challenge. To minister to people in this way is a demanding responsibility.

In James 1:2, he says, "My brethren, count it all joy when you fall into divers temptation;" (King James). In The Living Bible, it says, "Dear brothers, is your life full of difficulties and temptations? Then be happy, for when the way is rough, your patience has a chance to grow" (verses 3-4).

In II Peter 5:8, we are told the devil, as a roaring lion, prowls around looking for someone to devour. My point in this: Satan doesn't waste his time trying to bring down the man on the bottom. It's the one at the top he's after. The fact that we are being hindered is evidence that we are doing what is right. If we were not doing anything, the devil would leave us alone.

Is not this one of the great truths of the book of Job? "Hast thou considered my servant Job? For there is none like him in all the earth!" (American Standard Version - Job 1:8). Satan spared no strength to attempt to capture Job's soul. God allowed the temptation for a reason.

Satan powerfully came to Jesus at the beginning of His ministry. After Jesus overcame, he left Him only temporarily.

"But we have one that has been tempted in every way" (Heb. 4:15).

But Paul makes it very plain in I Corinthians 10:13,

". . .but God is faithful, who will not suffer you to be tempted above that you are able; but will with the temptation also make a way of escape. . ." (King James Version).

The great truth to remember in the face of trial and temptation is - God is in control. He will temper our burdens to our ability to bear them.

Perhaps the absence of such temptation may be an indication of one of two things. You are not strong enough to withstand the temptation, and the Lord is indeed giving you what you can bear. The absence of great temptation may also mean you are at the bottom of the ladder, safe in the devil's grip; he has no time for you until you start doing something right, so sleep on!

Now, what about a church? Does this apply? Sure! If you are dead in the woods, what difference does it make? If you are on the front line of a real battle for God, then that is a threat. Satan will attack with his big guns. Who will he use? The people with influence. What will he do? Divide and conquer. Split your church, your home, your family, your heart. Deception is his thing. Find people with influence, appeal to their ego! Evil heart: Jealousy! Whatever - it doesn't matter. Just divide and conquer. Destroy it before it destroys you. To the victor belongs the spoils!

How often God tries to warn us to watch our own steps, to save us from stepping into trouble. How often we go about our business, not hearing, not listening, not responding.

Some Christians have segregated their lives into spiritual and secular compartments, and it depends upon who they are with, or where they are, as to which compartment they are in. It is difficult, however, to hide really true Christian character. Character is like a tree and reputation is like its shadow. The shadow is what we think of it. The tree is what it is. Your reputation is not determined by what you do. Your reputation is determined by what people think about what you do. When you allow the wrong thing to be concluded from your actions, though your heart may be as pure as the morning dew, you have made a serious and bad mistake. If you are a leader in the Lord's church, you hurt the whole leadership by allowing questions to arise as to your actions. People oftentimes not only look at what you do, but search for motives which caused your actions, the scene behind the scene.

A true leader is likely to be one who has no desire to lead, but is forced into that position of leadership by the pressure of the congregation and the work of the Holy Spirit. Such were Moses and David. I think there was hardly a great leader, from Paul to the present day, that was not drafted by the Holy Spirit for the task commissioned by the Lord. I believe it might be accepted as a work of God for an elder, deacon or preacher to admit to himself that God has placed him there for a purpose, and then pray daily to find and fulfill that purpose.

Criticism will come, but that can be used as an asset, if the heart is right before God. The popularity of an individual leader can create a problem. His feeling of superiority or infallibility, especially in his decision making ability, can create a problem. His certainty that he is indispensable, and that the church without him could not survive, can create a problem. Pride and egotism can create a problem in leadership that is most difficult with which to work. The simple truth is that some people cannot handle power. It goes to their head. They become exacting and demanding, uncooperative and unforgiving. They assume positions that are not theirs to take. But as we all know, it is easier to put an elder in office than it is to get him out. It is easier to tear down than it is to build. It is easier to discourage than it is to encourage. Leadership can suffer because of lack of encouragement.

It is a very dangerous thing to lose sight of the eternal in our race for the material. It matters little how much a man is worth when weighed on financial scales; all of it will be pried from his cold, dead hand and be given to another. The world will soon forget the fame we have won, and the ribbons and medals. The world will soon be chasing another butterfly. It is how tall a man stands among his fellows - and how straight he stands - that leaves an empty place against the sky when he falls, like a mighty oak in the forest.

There have been men in the Restoration Movement who can never be totally forgotten. Some of them hammered out the Restoration concept, and others kept that concept clear and focused, allowing neither their adversaries nor their friends to turn them to either the right or to the left. If one is remembered with more gratitude than the other, it will be the man who held a straight course through currents and tides, crosswinds and undertows.

Churches of Christ are unique. There is no hierarchy; no centralized government of the body that forces congregations into line. Each is independent and autonomous. Whatever influence is exercised over the "brotherhood" is exercised by the strength of character, rather than political pull. This is the most dangerous of all things. It makes it possible for an unscrupulous man to take a segment of the church with him, if they are willing to follow the man; and he is willing to be their leader. It makes the church at his mercy, if he finds reason to lead a split. It is a safety feature in another way; just as the plurality of elders in a local church is a safety feature. There is more security in a multitude of counsel, than in a dictator. The most dangerous thing that could possibly happen is for a brotherhood savior to arise, who thinks he has all the right answers and that everyone else is going to hell. May God have mercy on him and all those who choose to follow him. Search our history and you will find that every split, and every satanic division in the church, has been the result of some preacher, elder or editor, who loved the preeminence. The church will always owe a great debt of gratitude to an elder or preacher who steers a straight course in the heat of battle, one who, among his siblings, shows love and concern for that which is God's.

To serve in the capacity of elder or preacher in the church he must be able to stand the heat in the kitchen, without even perspiring. He has to keep his head clear when those about him are losing theirs and blaming it on him. Those who can't do it have to get out. A real giant shows his strength when he is pressured. It takes a big, big man to continue quietly on his determined course with little dogs nipping constantly at his heels. Some leaders lead by the noise they make; the real ones by the course they take.

The brotherhood will always owe a debt of gratitude to those in whom the qualities of real leadership loom large. Real leaders are scarce and we miss them when they go. It is to be devoutly hoped that their greatest contribution may be the inspiration they give to younger men to even surpass them in the age to come. The Kingdom must spread and grow strong; and without big men, it can't.

There are two groups of siblings usually found in the church: those who are involved in some effort, and those who are alarmed about it. Those who are for it and those who are against it. Each is probably a balance for the other. It is regrettable that certain human factors have made some brethren demand a "split" of the local congregation. Some of them talk of the "division" they have caused without a shred of shame. What a shame that we spend our energies in an effort to annihilate, rather than to build up. Yet, when the warnings of the conscientiously concerned are completely ignored, what more can you do?

The church is not a social crusading body. It is God-directed rather than human-directed, and the scriptures are the basis for what comes from the pulpit or the class room. God knows we are not working against each other; we are working with each other. To make the church more the Church of Christ, the Body of Christ, the Family of God; that is where we should be going. That can't be if all we do is bad-mouth each other and fight each other.

If there is a basic characteristic of the church of Christ, which stands out above all others, it is the acceptance of the Bible as the only source of revealed truth. The church today is caught in the fast current of changing social order. There is a restlessness among us that I have never seen before. Some are saying it is because the "Baby Boomers" have come of age, and now must be dealt with. Maybe that is part of it, but the worst problem is an unwillingness to accept authority. This is true in the marriage relationship (so we just walk off, get a divorce, and forget it), or we kill the lawman because he is trying to tell us what to do, or we reject the leadership of the church and walk off, either going somewhere else or not at all.

We are "the ekklesia," the called out of God. It is not enough to just belong, we must commit. We must become the people after God's very own heart. This can never be if we are head strong at being a people determined to do as we please. Where is the authority for that?

The moment of truth comes to all of us at one time or another. When a very specially bred bull trots into the arena, he encounters the matador who uses a large cape to execute a series of provocative actions to induce the bull to charge. When this is accomplished, the bull, in a rather unknowing way, causes his own death. The lances are placed with power into the neck and the shoulders of the infuriated animal. The bull makes his final charge; the matador waits until he is

almost upon him, then leaps to the
left, lunging over the right horn and
driving the sword deep into the heart
and lungs of the animal. His wishes
are to produce instantaneous death.
This climatic moment is called "the moment of truth." It is the instant of
peril when the bull, by the slightest
upward toss of his head, can gore the
body of the man, and cause his agoniz-
ing death. The moment of truth is when
one man pits his all - his life, his
fortune and his sacred honor - on the
outcome of a single thrust. WHY? SO
WHAT? HOW COME? Because a man has got
to do what a man has got to do. It may
seem so useless to others as to why
people do what they do. Deep in the
heart of all of us lies the drive that
causes us to climb the mountain, and
the only reason we can offer is because
it is there and I must climb it.

The moment of truth for Christians
among their siblings is that, regardless of hurt, conflict, embarrassment,
humiliation, hate or jealousy, we must
forgive that we might be forgiven.

He, who refuses to forgive, burns
the bridge over which one day he must
travel.